JUAN LUIS VIVES

IN PSEUDODIALECTICOS

A CRITICAL EDITION

STUDIES
IN MEDIEVAL AND
REFORMATION THOUGHT

EDITED BY

HEIKO A. OBERMAN, Tübingen

IN COOPERATION WITH

E. JANE DEMPSEY DOUGLASS, Claremont, California
LEIF GRANE, Copenhagen
GUILLAUME H. M. POSTHUMUS MEYJES, Leiden
ANTON G. WEILER, Nijmegen

VOLUME XXVII

CHARLES FANTAZZI Ed.

JUAN LUIS VIVES

IN PSEUDODIALECTICOS

A CRITICAL EDITION

LEIDEN
E. J. BRILL
1979

JOANNES LUDOVICUS VIVES
VALENTINUS.

JUAN LUIS VIVES

IN PSEUDODIALECTICOS

A CRITICAL EDITION

INTRODUCTION, TRANSLATION AND COMMENTARY

BY

CHARLES FANTAZZI

LEIDEN
E. J. BRILL
1979

This book has been published with the help of a grant from the Canadian Federation for the Humanities, using funds provided by the Social Sciences and Humanities Research Council of Canada.

ISBN 90 04 05977 6

PRINTED IN THE NETHERLANDS

CONTENTS

TABLE OF CONTENTS

PREFACE

With such huge undertakings as the Yale edition of the works of Thomas More, the Amsterdam critical edition of Erasmus, and the Toronto *Collected Works of Erasmus* project now well under way, it seems to be the propitious moment to make some small beginning in the *opus* of their younger contemporary, Juan Luis Vives. Although perhaps not of their stature, this much neglected Spanish humanist remains a very important figure, together with Erasmus, More and Budé, in the Northern Renaissance republic of letters. His critical approach to ancient and modern writers, his important contributions to pedagogy, law and medicine, and his pioneering work in psychology and social reform, far in advance of his time, mark him out as a truly original thinker. Less vitriolic than most of his fellow humanists, and less aloof from the cares of the common people, he holds a special charm for the modern reader.

The youthful diatribe against the logicians of Paris is in many respects a mere reiteration of traditional humanist ridicule of the strange language and behavior of that despised breed of professionals. It differs significantly, however, in the fact that the author, a fresh product of the schools himself, shows much more understanding of their doctrine than other indignant but less well-informed scoffers. Despite its importance, no critical edition of this work is currently available. In a collection of translations entitled *Renaissance Philosophy* (The Hague, 1972) I provided a tentative English version of this essay, which has been radically revised and expanded for the present edition, and provided with an introduction and full commentary.

For photocopies and microfilms I am indebted to the Biblioteca Nacional of Madrid, and the Biblioteca Menéndez y Pelayo of Santander. A microfilm from the latter library was procured for me through the kind instrumentality of Professor Antonio Fontán of the Universidad Autónoma of Madrid. I owe special gratitude to Professor Paul Vincent Spade of the University of Indiana for his expert guidance through the tangles of sophistic argumentation. His long epistle was a worthy rejoinder in defense of the philosophers to the monitory letter of Vives to his friend, Juan

Fort. I am obliged also to Professor Norman Kretzmann of Cornell University for the elucidation of several recalcitrant sophisms, and to my colleague, Professor Ralph Johnson, for his careful critique of the philosophical introduction. To Professor Heiko Oberman of Tübingen I should like to express my gratitude for his acute observations on the manuscript and for his acceptance of the study in the series directed by him. I am most grateful to the University of Windsor for a generous grant in aid of publication from its humanities research fund.

THE TEXT

The only readily available edition of the complete writings of Luis Vives is that published from 1782 to 1790 by the Valencian humanist, Gregorio Mayáns y Siscar, under the patronage of the Archbishop of Valencia, Don Francisco Fabian y Fuero. The eight volumes of this edition, *J. L. Vivis Valentini Opera Omnia*, reprinted in 1964 by the Gregg Press in London, is a faulty reproduction of the *editio princeps* of the complete works printed in Basel in 1555 by Nicolaus Episcopius, or Nicolas l'Evesque le Jeune, which already contained its own share of errors.

In the case of the *In pseudo-dialecticos* there is extant an edition published in Louvain by Thierry Martens of Alost, which contains no date in the colophon, but does bear the date 13 February, 1519 at the end of the letter, as in all the editions. There seems to be no doubt that this date is to be considered Old Style, and therefore really 1520. This is confirmed by the letter of Vives to Erasmus, telling of his friendly reception in Paris, which can be dated to around June 4, 1520. (Allen, *Opus Epistolarum Des. Erasmi Roterodami*, IV, ep. 1108).[1] The chronology given by Allen is based in this instance on the Froben edition of Erasmus' correspondence, and is confirmed by the secure knowledge of the comings and goings during those days of Budé, whom Vives met in this visit to Paris, and also by the accurate chronicling of the controversy concerning the lectures of William Nesen at Louvain.[2] In both letters of Erasmus in response to Vives, reference is made to this incident as if it were past history, and it is known that Nesen had been residing in the Lily at Louvain since July, 1519, and did not return to Germany until July of the following year. Vives himself was also involved in this dispute, and it may be deduced from Erasmus' words that there were still very tangible repercussions of the affair in Louvain. Vives' lively description of his feelings of uneasiness in the presence of the Parisian scholars makes it clear

---

[1] Old Style dates are the norm for Martens' books as they appear in Nijhoff-Kronenberg, *Nederlandsche Bibliographie van 1500 tot 1540* (The Hague, 1923).

[2] For detailed and specific data concerning the injunction against Nesen, cf. Henri de Vocht, *History of the Foundation and Rise of the Collegium Trilingue Lovaniense, Humanistica lovaniensia*, 10, (1951), pp. 453-469.

that his letter to Fort had been circulated very recently, and that
he was expecting a hostile reception. He states that he attempted
unsuccessfully to avoid the subject, but that Fort, unable to
contain himself any longer, broached the matter to the amusement
of all present, and it was apparent from their reaction that Vives
had been acquitted of any blame, as it were. Indeed, according
to his account, they confessed that they had taken his words in
good part and were grateful to him for his efforts to confute this
madness propagated by the sophists. Whether we are to take
Vives' report to Erasmus at his word or not, it is certainly clear
that his invective was still fresh in the minds of his hearers, and
the date of the treatise must be given as 1520, not 1519.

The treatise figures as the last, and therefore probably the most
recent, of a long list of opuscula in the Louvain edition. It is the
companion piece to the *Pompeius fugiens* in an edition printed by
Lazare Schürer in Sélestat, or Schlettstadt, for which we have a
definite date, 1520, as given in the colophon:

SELESTADII IN AEDIBUS
Lazari Schurerii Mense Iunio
M.D.XX.

It is simply impossible on the strength of the available evidence to
determine which edition was authorized by Vives himself, or which
was prior in time. In the case of Vives, we are not so fortunate as
to have the records of the progress and surveillance of the printing
as we do in the correspondence of Erasmus and More with Froben,
Badius Ascensius and other printers. I am inclined to believe that
Schürer printed a version in which some final revisions and corrections had not yet been made. In collating these two earliest
editions, I have found that there are some slight stylistic variations
and occasional rhetorical amplifications in the Sélestat printing.
The stylistic corrections often involve some nicety of the sub-
junctive versus a more straightforward indicative, and in all cases
the Louvain reading is preferable. At other times it is merely a
question of an inconsequential difference in word order, an addi-
tional adjective, or a second, reinforcing verb. An already exces-
sively lengthy list of sophisms is further and rather otiosely aug-
mented in this edition. Vives had already made his point, advancing
the argument to a *reductio ad absurdum*, so that the addition of
more letters of the alphabet arranged in the form of impossible

and unintelligible syllogisms is entirely superfluous, and in fact, detracts from the efficacy of the examples. The Sélestat text also exhibits several instances of decidedly inferior usage as well as a few patent grammatical errors. A line concerning the forceful expulsion of the sophists from Paris is omitted in this edition, one wonders by whom, author or editor.

The Louvain edition has the greater claim to authenticity in that the piece was written in Louvain, and Vives obviously would have had easier access to the printer, Thierry Martens, and could have personally supervised the printing. At any rate, the Louvain edition is the basis of a 1538 edition printed at Basel, hence in Vives' lifetime and subject to his approval, which is in turn exactly identical with the 1555 *editio princeps* of Episcopius. I have thus chosen this as the basis of my text, relegating to the apparatus the variants of the Sélestat edition as well as some minor erroneous readings that crept into the Mayáns text. The punctuation of the latter is particularly erratic and incorporates peculiarly Spanish characteristics like the inverted question and exclamation marks, and bizarre paragraphing. I have adhered essentially to the punctuation and capitalization of the 1555 Basel edition, even where it seemed a bit excessive, as in the setting off of all relative clauses. In these, as in other accidentals, I have followed the example of the Yale edition of the works of St. Thomas More. Most of the orthographic inconsistencies typical of Renaissance Latin have been reduced to the norm, after the example of Remigio Sabbadini's edition of the letters of Guarino and Alessandro Perosa's exemplary text of the poems of Marullo, while still reflecting certain peculiarities of the author. V's have been made into u's, except as majuscules, j's are printed as i's, and s is printed for long s. I have also retained the qu for c in words like *quum* and *loquuntur*. The genitive in *ae* is always used whenever an *e* is found in the basic text. Ordinary contractions, save for ampersands, are silently expanded. All variants are recorded, except for simple interchangeable spellings.

I have adhered to the clean, unencumbered format of the Yale edition of Thomas More, in which the lemma is followed by a bracket, the variant reading or readings and the sigla, which for the *In pseudo-dialecticos* are as follows:

L, Louvain, Thierry Martens, 1520
S, Sélestat, Lazare Schürer, 1520
B, Basel, Nicolas l'Evesque, 1555
V, Valencia, Mayáns y Siscar, 1782-90

As for the title, I have reported the various forms in the apparatus as they are given in the early editions. The *editio princeps* of Basel, which I follow in most other respects, has *In pseudo-dialecticos Liber*, but I have preferred to omit the last word, in order to preserve the title by which the treatise is most commonly known.

INTRODUCTION

While the Aragonese court in Naples under Alfonso V, el Mag-
nánimo,[1] was the scene of an initial burgeoning of the new learning
among Spanish thinkers, the full impact of the Renaissance was
not felt in Spain itself until the 16th century. Its chief luminary is
without a doubt the Valencian, Juan Luis Vives, one of the greatest
intellectual figures of the Renaissance. He was born in Valencia
of a Jewish family, a recurrent *punctum dolens* for Spanish his-
torians,[2] in 1492, year of the *Reconquista*. By the age of fourteen
Vives was enrolled in the *Estudio General* of Valencia, where he
studied Latin grammar under Daniel Sisó and Jerónimo Amiguet.
The latter is described as 'homo insigniter barbarus' by Mayáns
in his biography of Vives,[3] who supports his choice of epithet with
a story concerning Vives' early school days, first recounted in
Gaspar Escolano's *Décadas de la Historia de Valencia*, written in
1611. It seems that some Valencian scholars were in favor of intro-
ducing the radical pedagogical ideas of Antonio de Nebrija [4] into
the school curriculum, an innovation to which Amiguet was
staunchly opposed. In reaction to this proposed move, Amiguet
had his most eloquent pupil compose a speech against the introduction of these new grammatical theories.[5] Vives was later to

---

[1] One of the best accounts of this period is still Benedetto Croce, *La
corte spagnuola di Alfonso d'Aragona a Napoli*, Atti dell'Accademia Pontiana
vol. XXIV (Naples, 1894).

[2] The great Spanish savant, Menéndez y Pelayo, was reluctant to admit to
the Jewish extraction of Vives, while the editor and translator of his works,
Lorenzo Riber, dismisses the probability of a "tacha ancestral" ("ancestral
blemish") in such a "debelador de musulmanes y judíos". *Juan Luis Vives
Obras Completas*, ed. Lorenzo Riber (Madrid, 1947), I. p. 15. Documentation
concerning Vives' family may be found in Miguel Pinta y Florente, and
José M. de Palacio *Procesos inquisitoriales contro la familia judía de Luis
Vives* (Madrid, 1964).

[3] "Vivis Vita", in *J. L. Vivis Valentini Opera Omnia*, ed. Gregorio Mayáns
y Siscar (Valencia, 1782-1790), vol. I, p. 20. This edition will be cited
hereafter by the Latinized form of the editor's name, Majansius.

[4] In 1522 Vives was offered the prestigious chair of rhetoric at the University of Alcalá, to succeed the famous Nebrija. The offer was made by Juan
de Vergara, who had himself declined the honor in favor of Vives. Cf. the
letter of Vergara to Vives and the official letter of the University in A.
Bonilla y San Martín, *Clarorum Hispaniensium epistolae ineditae* in *Revue
Hispanique* 8 (1901), pp. 73-74 and 86-87.

[5] The incident is related in Majansius, "Vivis Vita", I, 16-18.

retract this adolescent defense of linguistic barbarism in his *De causis corruptarum artium*,[6] and gave frequent praise to Nebrija's writings in his own pedagogical treatises.

In 1509 Vives set out for the University of Paris, joining many other Spanish and, in particular, Valencian students in the Faculty of Arts and that of Theology. He resided at Montaigu College, proverbial for its almost monastic discipline and scholastic orientation,[7] and was enrolled in the Faculty of Arts, where, owing to his previous grounding in Latin grammar and rhetoric, he was admitted immediately into the intricacies of formal logic and dialectic. His teachers were the Belgian logician, John Dullært, and the Aragonese scholar, Gaspar Lax de Sariñena. Later Vives would provide a vivid, firsthand account of student life in Paris at that time in the simulated dialogues of the *Exercitatio linguæ latinæ*, a very entertaining manual that has nothing of the vehement invective of the *In pseudo-dialecticos*.

In 1512 Vives left Paris, disillusioned by his experience there, and moved on to the city of Bruges where he would live almost uninterruptedly until 1517. He became a tutor to the children of Bernard Valdaura, a wealthy merchant of the flourishing Spanish community of that city.

In the spring of 1514 the young scholar returned to Paris, as we learn from a letter addressed to the same Juan Fort to whom the *In pseudo-dialecticos* is dedicated. The letter accompanies an edition of Hyginus, a Latin writer on astronomy much in favor at the time. Vives intended to use this text in public lectures at Paris, as he tells his friend.[8] It is interesting that even in this earlier letter to Fort Vives exhorts his friend to put aside for a few days at least the quibblings of Swineshead and the minute distinctions of Gaspar Lax. A fortnight later, on Easter Day, the same professor invited Vives, Fort and some other Valencian students to have dinner with him in his room at Montaigu College. From this meeting Vives fashioned the setting of his devotional dialogue, *Christi Iesu*

---

[6] Majansius, VI, 325-26.

[7] The regimen of abstinence and silence, and in particular, the unsavoury meals served to the students at Montaigu College, inspired Erasmus' satiric *Ichthyophagia*. For a fuller description of the school see Chapter II "The College de Montaigu" in George Faludy, *Erasmus of Rotterdam* (London, 1970), pp. 49-72.

[8] Majansius, IV, 420.

Triumphus et Mariæ parentis eius Ovatio, published by the same Parisian printer, Jehan Lambert, who had produced the Hyginus.

Apart from this brief sojourn in Paris and some time passed in Brussels and Louvain, Bruges remained the city of his adoption, as he expresses openly in the preface to his *De subventione pauperum* (1526), addressed to the magistrates of that city.[9] A more permanent transferral to Louvain came as a result of Vives' being selected by Guillaume de Croy to be his private preceptor. The young noble had already been named Bishop of Cambrai at the age of nineteen, and was arch-bishop designate of Toledo, destined to succeed the famous Cardinal Cisneros. Through the patronage of his young ward, Vives enjoyed a certain prestige among the intellectual elite of the city and by special privilege was licensed to give public lectures without being on the official roster of the Brabant university.

Numerous short religious and philosophical writings issued from the pen of the Spanish humanist during this period, but it was the tract against the pseudo-dialecticians that brought him swiftly to the notice of the scholarly world. Thomas More, writing to Erasmus in the following year, after copies of Vives' books had been brought to him from Louvain, enthusiastically endorsed the forceful treatise and recognized the talent and enviable Latin style of the youthful Spanish scholar.[10] Erasmus answered in a tone of similar praise, "No other man is more fitted to put to rout the battalions of the dialecticians, in whose camp he served for many years." [11] In a letter of his own to Erasmus on the 4th of June 1520, Vives could report elatedly that in a short return visit to Paris he was accorded a friendly reception by the very "sophists" whom he had attacked.[12] Obviously in the few years that had intervened since his student days there, the sophists had relented considerably in their propagation of logical subtleties, although there were still some "doctors", as Vives writes, who contented their hearers with the traditional academic display of learning.

---

[9] The text of the letter is given in a recent article of prime importance for this early period of Vives' life, J. IJsewijn, "J. L. Vives in 1512-1517. A Reconsideration of Evidence", *Humanistica lovaniensia* XXVI (1977), 93.

[10] *Opus Epistularum Des. Erasmi Roterodami*, ed. P. S. Allen (Oxford, 1930-38), vol. IV, 1106, 20-108.

[11] "Non alius magis idoneus qui profliget sophistarum phalanges, in quorum castris diu meruerit." *Ibid.*, IV, 1107, 12-13.

[12] *Ibid.*, IV, 1108, 5-15.

At the behest of Erasmus, Vives began work in Louvain in 1520 on a commentary to Augustine's *City of God* to complement Erasmus' own critical revisions of the Augustinian corpus and to contribute to a larger scholarly project of emending the writings of the early Church Fathers. It was a huge undertaking, rendered more difficult by the absence of a reliable text and copies of the ancient authors to aid him in his tracing of Augustine's sources. This long and exhausting labor taxed the young man's delicate health, and strained his friendly relations with the older humanist, who proved to be a harsh and importunate critic of the work, as it progressed.[13] With the premature death in January, 1520 of his young charge, Guillaume de Croy, Vives was reduced to tutoring young Spanish boys in Louvain to supplement the meager income from his lectures in the halls of the university. A fruitful encounter, arranged by his friend, Francis Craneveldt,[14] was instrumental in delivering Vives from these financial difficulties. In August of 1520 in the Prinsenhof, the great palace of the Duke of Brabant, he was introduced to Thomas More, who had arrived in the company of Cardinal Wolsey on official embassy from Henry VIII. Perhaps it was at More's suggestion that Vives later dedicated his commentary to the English king, but neither Henry nor Catherine of Aragon was yet prepared to provide him with sufficient patronage for the life-long independent pursuit of his studies (ocium ad vitam studiosam, Allen, V, 1222, 17). When the chair of the controversial philologist, Antonio Nebrija, fell vacant at the University of Alcalà, Vives was offered this prestigious position. On May 10, 1523, he wrote to Craneveldt and Erasmus that he was to travel to Spain via England.[15]

---

[13] Actually these commentaries were a very significant contribution to the elucidation of Augustinian thought and were frequently reprinted both in the original Latin and in English and French versions. Erasmus seems to have been very disappointed in its commercial failure at the Frankfort Book Fair and criticized it for being too long and carelessly done. Allen, V, 1271 and 1351. The book was condemned by the theologians of Louvain in 1546 for its unorthodox views and was put on the Roman Index of Forbidden Books by Clement VIII in 1596: "Vives Valentini Annotationes in S. Augustinum nisi expurgentur", cf. Fr. Heinrich Reusch, *Die Indices librorum prohibitorum des sechzehnten Jahrhunaerts* (Tübingen, 1886; repr. De Graff, 1961), p. 562.

[14] The exchange of letters between the two humanists may be found in *Litterae virorum eruditorum ad Franciscum Craneveldium*, ed. Henri de Vocht (Louvain, 1929).

[15] *Ibid.*, Ep. 56 vv. 14-20; Allen, V, 1362, 102-105.

Once in the bustling Tudor metropolis, Vives never speaks again of his projected visit to Spain. Almost immediately he found entrance into university circles. It was the Chancellor of England himself, Cardinal Wolsey, who appointed Vives to a lectureship in his own foundation, the new Cardinal College, then housed in Oxford's Corpus Christi College. With the Cardinal's encouragement he effected various fundamental reforms of the curriculum,[16] and together with his friends, John Fisher, Thomas Linacre, and William Latimer, contributed greatly to the intellectual life of England of this period. For Queen Catherine he completed various educational works intended for the seven-year-old Princess Mary, including a plan of study, the *De ratione studii puerilis*, which he offered to her personally on her visit to Oxford to hear him lecture. He had previously dedicated to her a handbook on the upbringing of Christian women, which served as a kind of companion piece to Erasmus' *Education of a Christian Prince*. In addition to his professorial duties at Oxford Vives immediately became a kind of official spokesman for humanist ideas on the conduct of the state. The *De consultatione*, ostensibly a treatise on rhetorical deliberation, was in effect a political document, as were his translations of Isocrates' *Areopagitica oratio* and *Ad Nicoclen*, both of them dealing with the duties of monarchs, which he dedicated to Cardinal Wolsey.

Returning to the Lowlands in April 1524, Vives married Margarita Valdaura, the young daughter of Bernard Valdaura, at whose home he had been offered hospitality during his frequent visits to Bruges. The young spouse remained throughout their happy marriage the model of Christian womanhood envisioned by Vives in various treatises on the subject. During this same summer he wrote the beautiful spiritual and educational treatise, *Introductio ad sapientiam*,[17] in which he gives fervent expression to his lofty Christian ideals. To Princess Mary he also sent a shorter devotional work, the *Satellitium animi*, in which the mild message of Christ is implicitly set against the fierce emblems of kingship. In September of that same year Vives is again in England to resume lectures at the express wish of Cardinal Wolsey, and in the spring of the following year he

---

[16] The curriculum developments in these colleges are excellently discussed in ch. 4, "Humanism in the Universities 1500 to 1530", in James Kelsey McConica, *English Humanists and Reformation Politics under Henry VIII and Edward VI* (Oxford, 1965), pp. 76-105.

[17] This work has been translated into English, *Vives' Introduction to Wisdom, A Renaissance Textbook* by Marian Tobriner (New York, 1968).

returned once more to Bruges after the outbreak of the plague. From there in a letter dated Oct. 8, 1525, he addressed a fervent appeal to Henry to unite Christian princes in the face of the Turkish menace as Suleiman's troops advanced through western Hungary, but his pleas were ignored. By now Wolsey's attitude towards Vives had changed drastically. He favored France against Charles V, and thus Vives, now an open enemy in his attempts at conciliation, was abruptly dismissed from his lectureship.

During this stay in Bruges, Vives wrote his important tract, *De subventione pauperum*, addressed to the magistrates of his adopted city. No doubt his theories were influenced by social reforms then being instituted in the cities of Flanders as well as by the insights and analyses of More's *Utopia*. Indeed during the last month of his previous London sojourn, he was the guest of Thomas More at his home in Chelsea, and must have discussed these themes frequently with him. As in the *Utopia*, the first book of the treatise is theoretical, while the second gives concrete suggestions for social legislation to relieve the miseries of poverty. Vives expresses his particular concern for the plight of war victims, dispersed throughout Europe, who, he observes, should be accorded charitable hospitality and treated like native citizens. His enlightened attitude towards the poor, imbued with the principles of Christian charity, was far in advance of his time, and incurred the charge of heresy from Nicholas de Bureau, vicar-general of the diocese of Tournai.

In the spring of 1526 Vives was again in England (his many crossings prompted Erasmus to call him an amphibious animal), apparently still intent on persuading Henry to intercede on the side of peace. He returned to Bruges in May, greatly despondent in the face of the impending crisis and in October, 1526, wrote a dialogue on the dissension in Europe, *De Europæ dissidiis et bello turcico*. He proposes the obvious solution that Christians should unite under one leader instead of fighting among themselves.

By mid-April, 1527, Vives was back in England and, outwardly at least, the English monarchs remained cordial to him; he was even asked by the king to help in the preparation of a response to Luther's letter of Sept. 1, 1525. The illness and dejection of his wife, Margaret, prompted him to return once more to Bruges for a few months, until the queen asked him to return to England as the tutor of Princess Mary.

During this fifth stay in England Vives fell into the permanent
disfavor of Henry and Wolsey by his loyalty and counsel to the
queen in the famous marital situation obliquely referred to by
Erasmus in a letter to Vives as "the Jove and Juno affair".[18] The
Spanish humanist was subjected to house arrest through the
machinations of Wolsey. He was finally released after a period
of confinement lasting some thirty-eight days, and left England
at the advice of Catherine. She recalled him in November together
with two advocates from Flanders, but when she expressed dis-
pleasure at Vives' advice not to submit to the sham trial, he left
England forever.

Having failed in his role as pacifist with Henry, Vives turned to
the Emperor Charles V in 1529 in his *De concordia et discordia
humani generis*, voicing his despair of European civilization, newly
invigorated by the humanist revival, but now doomed by political
and social turmoil to be overthrown by the Turks. A somberly
realistic essay on Christian survival under the Turk accompanied
the longer work. Another essay, *De pacificatione*, was dispatched
a few weeks later to Alfonso Manrique, General Inquisitor of Spain,
as a sort of appendix to the previous work, suggesting practical
applications of his plans for peace.

The rest of Vives' life was spent in the Netherlands, mostly in
Bruges, except for frequent sojourns in Breda during the years
1537 and 1538, where he was charged with the humanistic education
of Doña Mencía de Mendoza, wife of the Duke of Nassau. Here he
published a commentary on Virgil's *Bucolics*, the *Interpretatio
allegorica in Bucolica Vergili*, and a very brief essay, *De Aristotelis
operibus censura*, reviewing the works of Aristotle, and warning
that one must be widely read to understand the master's writings.
An astonishing number of longer treatises on diverse subjects were
written in these later years. Of his pedagogical writings the twenty
books of the monumental *De disciplinis* appeared in 1531. This
extraordinary synthesis of the literary culture of his time has often
been considered a significant prelude to Bacon's *Instauratio*. The
first seven books on the corruption of learning are especially interesting for their continued criticism of philosophy and theology, en-
larging on the attacks of the *In pseudo-dialecticos*. He returns to
the attack against the blind followers of Aristotle, and advocates

---

[18] Allen, VII, 2040, 41-49.

the restoration of unadulterated Aristotelian logic. Of his other pedagogical writings, the *Exercitationes linguæ latinæ*, a witty collection of dialogues for the learning of Latin, became a standard textbook in European schools, going through fifty editions in the sixteenth century alone. Numerous *prælectiones* and commentaries on classical Latin authors, especially Cicero and Virgil, testify to the critical acumen and historical and empirical bent of his educational talents. Perhaps the most truly original and farseeing observations of the Spanish thinker are contained in his treatise, *De anima et vita*, which combines the wisdom of the ancient philosophers with his own empirical observations. The essay displays such fine insights into the nature of the mind and psycho-physical interaction as to be considered the first essay in modern psychology.[19] In the last two years of his life Vives worked on an apology for the Christian faith, the *De veritate fidei christianæ*, the culmination of his religious writings, which was published after his death. Affected by gout and nephritis, Vives died in the year 1540 and was buried in the chapel of St. Joseph in the church of St. Donatian in Bruges, destroyed during the time of the French Revolution. The simple altar inscription read as follows:

> Hier is begraven meester
> Jan Ludovicus Vives
> geboren van valencia in spagnien
> hie overleet
> anno MDXL den VI in meye.

Vives' youthful assault upon the Sorbonne logicians was a sort of self-purgation of the doctrines he had himself imbibed at the feet of the Parisian doctors, lessons which he found it difficult to unlearn, once they were inculcated. In this attack he clears the way, as it were, for his own educational reforms which he would outline in the *De disciplinis*. The form of the polemic follows a familiar pattern of anti-scholastic diatribe, which can be traced back at least as far as Petrarch.[20] The one aspect of the teaching of scholastic

---

[19] He is called the father of modern psychology by his English admirer, Foster Watson in an article bearing that title in *Psychological Review* 22 (1915), 333-353.

[20] Writing to Tommaso Caloria of Messina, Petrarch counselled him on how to counter a garrulous old dialectician, who could not be quieted. The humanist assured his Sicilian friend that when it comes to taking pen in hand, these loud disputants suddenly lose their tongues. Francesco Petrarca,

logic that was most open to ridicule, especially to those converted
to *bonæ litteræ* and the careful cultivation of the classical languages,
was the distorted form of Latin in which it was cast.[21] For the
formulation of their minute distinctions the logicians found it
necessary to create their own specialized vocabulary and to strain
the grammatical structure of the language to the limits of com-
prehensibility. Vives protests that Cicero and Aristotle were able
to explain the rules of logic in everyday Latin and Greek familiar
to all speakers of those languages. Of course, this is a bit of a sim-
plification, for both of these writers used somewhat specialized and
technical terms, and indeed Cicero found himself impeded in his
philosophical writings by the constraints of the inflexible Latin
grammar. It remains true, however, that the linguistic innovations
which these two classical writers introduced were as nothing
compared to the bizarre convolutions of the latter-day logicians.
In his adherence to the strict canons of grammar and style Vives is
a true successor of the Italian humanists, like Lorenzo Valla, Leonardo Bruni, Poliziano, and others, who never ceased to inveigh
against the perversions of the Latin language wrought by the
Parisian doctors. In the preface to his *Elegantiæ*, Valla had laid all
the blame for this upon the Gauls, as he referred to them, who had
taken the Capitoline by storm. Vives, like him, calls upon men of
letters to resist this flood of barbarism descending from the Seine
and defend decent Latinity against its impudent assailants.

Familiares, ed. Vittorio Rossi (Firenze, 1933), I, pp. 35-38. The letter,
dated March 12, 1335, is also found in English translation in *The Renaissance
Philosophy of Man*, ed. Cassirer, Kristeller and Randall (Chicago, 1948),
pp. 134-139.

[21] Cf. Leonardo Bruni, *Ad Petrum Paulum Histrum Dialogus*, in which he
berates the philosophers for uttering more solecisms than real words, and
marvels that they can claim to teach philosophy without knowing literature
("quos ego nequeo satis mirari, quo pacto philosophiam didicerint, cum
litteras ignorent; nam plures soloecismos quam verba faciunt cum
loquuntur"), *Prosatori latini del Quattrocento*, ed. Eugenio Garin (Milan,
1952), p. 54. Of course the logicians would "distinguish" the uses of language
quoad elegantium and *quoad loicam peritorum*, and thus defend their disregard
for the rules of rhetoric. The humanists, on the other hand, looked upon
their horrid jargon as a gothic assault upon the republic of letters, and
Valla in his *Dialecticae disputationes* called for a *repastinatio* or pruning of the
language of philosophy. Together with the Parisians, the "ultimi Britanni"
also came in for their share of abuse. Cf. Eugenio Garin, "La cultura fiorentina
nella seconda metà del '300 e i barbari britannici" in *La rassegna della
letteratura italiana* 64 (1960), 181-195.

At the same time Vives does not wish to involve his own compatriots at the University of Paris in his wholesale condemnation.
They could not be held to blame, he says, if by virtue of their
superior talents, they had become so adept in this corrupt learning.
As a distinguished alumnus of the school himself and pupil of one
of the most famous of the so-called barbarians, John Dullært of
Ghent, he had first-hand knowledge of the excesses of the logical
training. Indeed, in the dedicatory letter which he wrote for Vives'
Sullan Declamations of 1520,[22] Erasmus marvels how the young
scholar could so easily turn his talents from the sophistic disputations of the schools, in which he had no rival, to the more tranquil
domain of the humanities. During his days at the Sorbonne, the
young Vives had witnessed the fierce academic controversies that
raged between the humanists of Lemoine College and those who
advocated a revival of nominalism, like John Major, regent of the
College of Montaigu and teacher of Dullært. In those same years he
must have had some knowledge of the philosophical writings of
Jacques Lefèvre d'Etaples who had produced a new commentary
on the *Organon* [23] in an attempt to recover the true meaning of the
Aristotelian texts and purify them of the accumulated adulterations
of three centuries of scholastic wranglings. Vives insists on this
fidelity to the master throughout the tract and berates the logicians
for their ignorance of the authentic teachings of their model.

Despite his protestations of having been exposed to the *Sortes*
(scholastic shorthand for Socrates) and "asses" of the schools,
Vives remained essentially a *grammaticus*, a denomination which
in the Renaissance still retained its original meaning of teacher
and interpreter of the classical authors. In the second book of the
De causis corruptarum artium he recalls an admonition which
Dullært had given him in his student days, viz., that his humanistic
training would prove to be detrimental to his career as a dialectician
and theologian ('quanto eris melior grammaticus, tanto peior
dialecticus et theologus").[24] The theology in question is the *theologia*

---

[22] Majansius, II, 315-319.
[23] The second edition of this work appeared in Paris in 1510, and in 1508,
the year before Vives arrived in Paris, Lefèvre had published the *Dialectica*
of George of Trebizond, an important statement of the new humanistic
directions in the study of logic. For a lucid account of this "querelle",
cf. Cesare Vasoli, *La dialettica e la retorica dell'umanesimo* (Milan, 1968),
pp. 134 ff.
[24] Majansius, VI, 86.

disputatrix, the scientific discipline then current in the schools, couched in the subtle language of scholastic logic, not the devotional kind of theological writing in which Vives was engaged.

The Spanish humanist does not argue for an elegant Latin, embellished with every rhetorical device, but for a mere naturalness of language to counter the complexities flaunted by the virtuosos of the schools. Men so versed in the subtleties of the Latin tongue as Vives and Erasmus found it intolerable that this noble vehicle of expression should be wilfully defiled and obfuscated to purvey what they considered to be a denaturalized form of knowledge. In the clever and forceful rhetoric of the tract itself Vives provides a fine example of the expository virtues of the Latin language which he extolled. The pretentious demeanor of the doctors, cloaked and bearded and mumbling their private lingo, was the object of the unceasing ridicule of the humanists. In no other of his extant works, distinctive among humanistic writings for their moderation, does the Spanish scholar, whose motto was "sine querela", indulge in such acrid polemics. It was for a good cause, the freeing of higher learning from the trammels and aridities of a fossilized system of learning, which no longer had anything to do with life or reality. Erasmus had poured his scorn upon them through the voice of Folly, who exhorts that "an entire regiment of sophists be enlisted to fight the Turks and Saracens rather than those armies of dull-witted soldiers",[25] while Vives' jibes at these curious creatures emerging awkwardly from the "Cimmerian darkness" and Gothic smog of the University of Paris into the world of everyday life anticipate the more gross satire later to be levelled at the denizens of the Sorbonne by Rabelais.

Vives reserved some choice salvos for one whom he considered especially responsible for the corruption of the Latin language and the perversion of the discipline of logic, the 13th century logician and physician, Peter of Spain, actually a Lusitanian from Lisbon, later to become Pope John XXI.[26] His *Summulæ logicales*, a compilation of Aristotelian doctrine, was the standard textbook

---

[25] Erasmus, *Praise of Folly* trans. Betty Radice (Harmondsworth, 1971), p. 161.

[26] This identification is now universally accepted. Cf. the edition of the *Tractatus* by L. M. de Rijk (Assen, 1972) p. xl. It was he who commissioned Etienne Tempier, bishop of Paris, to investigate the teachings of the radical Aristotelians of the University of Paris.

in logic through the fifteenth century.[27] The last six or seven
tracts of this work,[28] commonly referred to as the *Parva logicalia*,
or *Little Logicals*, formed the basis of the beginning course in logic,
and introduced the student to the elaborate, abstract vocabulary
that so incensed the humanists. The text held such a monopoly in
the curriculum that first-year students at Paris were surnamed
Summulistæ,[29] initiates, so to speak, in the mysteries of Peter of
Spain. Vives, as Thomas More had done before him in his letter
to Martin Dorp, liked to ridicule the title of the treatise, which
derives its name, both writers insist, from the fact that it contained
'little logic'.[30]

These last six tracts provide a compendious discussion of that
distinctly medieval contribution to the science of logic which went
by the name of the 'logic of the moderns' or *logica moderna*. The
main doctrine of this branch of the subject was the properties of
terms (*proprietates terminorum*), a study which was intended to
instill a mastery of the semantic and syntactic subtleties of language for use in sophistic debate. Up until about the middle of the
twelfth century the only works of Aristotle available to the Western
world were Boethius' translations, with commentary, of the *Categories* and the *On Interpretation*, Porphyry's *Isagoge* to the *Categories*, and some original treatises by Boethius. Of the four "missing"
books of the *Organon* that were re-discovered, it was the *On So-*

---

[27] One can derive some notion of the incredible diffusion of this text
from the number of extant and commentaries. Mullaly lists one hundred
and sixty-six in his bibliography. Joseph Mullaly *The Summulae Logicales
of Peter of Spain* (Notre Dame, 1945), pp. 133-158. The universality of his
fame is attested to by his presence in the second circle of lights in the *Paradiso*:
(Canto XII, 134-135). "Pietro Ispano/ lo qual giù luce in dodici libri". His
text was used in the Universities of Paris, Vienna, Cologne, Freiburg,
Leipzig, Ingolstadt and Tübingen, to mention only some of the main centers
of learning which adopted his teachings. We are told by the famous Chancellor of Paris, Jean de Gerson, that the young scholars were made to commit
his text to memory although they were not yet capable of understanding it.

[28] The authenticity of the seventh tract on exponibles, included by Mullaly,
is refuted in de Rijk's edition, *op. cit.*, p. lv, and is also omitted in Bochenski's
edition of the *Summulae* (Turin, 1947).

[29] Thus we are informed by Ramus in his *Scholae in liberales artes* (1569)
col. 1049, referred to by Walter Ong, *Ramus, Method and the Decay of Dialogue* (Cambridge, Mass., 1958), p. 58.

[30] "Now this book, the *Little Logicals*, which is so called, I suppose,
because it has very little logic in it. . ." *Sir Thomas More, Selected Letters*
ed. Elizabeth Frances Rogers (New Haven, 1961), p. 20. In an alternate reading of the text of Vives, the adjective is twisted from *parva* into *prava*,
"depraved". Cf. p. 26.

phistical Refutations which most caught the imagination of medieval thinkers [31] and led to the elaboration of the study of fallacies, and a new science of sophistic.[32] Thus students in the first year of philosophy spent their time sharpening their wits with myriad distinctions and endless quibbling instead of attending to the higher concerns of philosophy or even of logic. This training prepared them for subtle disputation in the art of dialectic rather than logic, although these two terms were often used interchangeably, especially by the humanist critics of the art, as in Vives' title.[33] Peter of Spain's widely quoted definition in the opening sentence of his treatise testifies to the privileged status of this subject: "Dialectica est ars artium et scientia scientiarum ad omnium methodorum principia viam habens." "Dialectic is the art of arts and the science of sciences, and it is the path to the basic principles of all methods." [34]

The most conspicuous exercise in the skills of this dialectic was the detection of the truth or falsity of certain ambiguous propositions known as sophisms. They were somewhat like the fallacious arguments discussed in Aristotle's *On Sophistical Refutations* in that the fallacy involved in each instance bore a deceptive resemblance to a valid argument. On one level the sophism could be judged true by means of an apparently correct argumentation, or alternately could be proved false by another equally cogent form of reasoning. The disputant, as the word implies etymologically, was to prune the subject under discussion of all falsity, and demonstrate that one or the other of two apparently acceptable solutions was in fact fallacious. By the ingenious manipulation of groups of grammatical modifiers, called syncategorematic terms, they were able to create fine linguistic and logical distinctions to bewilder their opponent.

Of the multiple properties of terms defined by the medieval

---

[31] L. M. de Rijk, *Logica Modernorum*, Vol. I (Assen, 1967) pp. 14-15.

[32] "Sophistic, or the study of sophisms, invited philosophers to exercise their ingenuity in making and solving new puzzles." William and Martha Kneale, *The Development of Logic* (Oxford, 1962) p. 227.

[33] Cf. Ong, *op. cit.*, p. 42: "The equation of dialectic and logic, which Ramus goes to such lengths here to explain, is simply what he and tens of thousands of other first-year philosophy students had soaked up, directly or indirectly, from the opening of Peter of Spain's *Summulae Logicales*."

[34] I cite the usual form of this definition, as it was generally known in the Middle Ages, although de Rijk rejects the extravagant superlatives, "ars artium et scientia scientiarum" in his critical edition.

logicians, the theory of supposition is of central importance. In his treatise on suppositions, Peter of Spain carefully distinguishes this term from signification.[35] The latter he defines as the representation of a thing through the imposition of a word, whereas supposition is defined as the acceptance of a term, already having meaning, to denote something. Etymologically, the medieval coinage *suppositio* means 'to stand for' or 'be placed for', and it is precisely this analysis of the ways in which words, occurring in a proposition, are used to stand for some thing or things, and affect the meanings of other words that constitutes the Parisian training in logic. De Rijk has shown how this development of medieval logic stemmed from the gradual shift in interest on the part of the late Latin grammarians from the inventions and impositions of individual words to their function (*vis et officium*) in the sentence.[36] As the grammarians had concerned themselves with the contextual importance of words, so the logicians stressed the functioning or properties of terms as part of a proposition. The terminology and subdivisions of this complex aspect of medieval logic vary from author to author, so that Peter of Spain, for example, differs considerably from William of Sherwood, who probably had written his treatise only a few years previously.[37] The latter philosopher, to cite one instance, restricted the property of supposition to subject terms only, saying that terms in predicate position have the property of 'copulation' rather than that of supposition.

Without attempting to enter here into all the intricacies of the subject, which would require a lengthy and complicated discussion, it would be useful to mention the main subdivisions of the term, as they are outlined in the *Summulæ*, in order that we may understand Vives' allusions to his sources. Schematically, they could be set out as follows: [38]

---

[35] *Tractatus*, ed. de Rijk, p. 80, 1.10. This distinction was first elaborated by the *moderni* who also gave currency to the term *suppositio*. De Rijk, *Logica Modernorum*, vol. II, Part I, pp. 123-24.

[36] L. M. de Rijk, *Logica Modernorum*, Vol. I, p. 117 ff.

[37] For the relative dates of the works of Sherwood, Peter of Spain and Lambert of Auxerre see *William of Sherwood's Introduction to Logic* ed. Norman Kretzmann (Minneapolis, 1966) pp. 4-5.

[38] This scheme is given in the *Summulae logicales*, ed. I. M. Bochenski (Rome, 1947), 6.04. It will be noted that Peter of Spain omits material supposition, or the mere matter of a word (i.e. its sound), as in the much-used example: "Sortes est dictio dyssyllaba."

Suppositio $\begin{cases} \text{discreta} \\ \text{communis} \end{cases}$ $\begin{cases} \text{naturalis} \\ \text{accidentalis} \end{cases}$ $\begin{cases} \text{simplex} \\ \text{personalis} \end{cases}$ $\begin{cases} \text{determinata}\,[39] \\ \text{confusa} \end{cases}$

Discrete supposition refers to the restricting of the discussion to one individual and unique thing to the exclusion of all others, denoted by a proper noun or a common noun with a limiting particle, usually the demonstrative pronoun 'this'. General terms which are not so restricted were said to have common supposition, which was then divided into two kinds, natural and accidental. A term possesses natural supposition when it refers to everything of which it is able to be predicated, as 'man' can stand for all mankind, who are, who have been, and who will be, as in the proposition 'Omnis homo est mortalis', where the verb is used in an omnitemporal sense. In accidental supposition, the same term would be modified according to its adjuncts, i.e. what is added to it, as in 'a man exists', in which the indefinite article limits it to one of presently existing men. Simple accidental supposition is defined as the acceptance of a general term for the universal thing signified by that term, as in the statement, 'Man is a species', i.e., man in general, not any particular man included in the term. The most usual type of supposition is personal, in which the term stands also for its particulars or inferiors, as in 'Man runs', i.e., 'man' may be Socrates or Plato or any individual man. This category is further divided into determinate and confused, and here the distinctions become more subtle. Peter of Spain, following William of Sherwood closely in this respect, defines determinate supposition as the acceptance of a general term expressed indefinitely or with a sign of particularity, as 'a man runs' (*homo currit*). He goes on to explain at some length that although the term 'man' may "suppose" or denote any man, running or non-running, the statement is asserted as true only of the one man who runs, and therefore 'man' stands determinately. Actually, this category of supposition was made necessary by a defect of the Latin language. Its lack of an indefinite article resulted in the ambiguity of such a phrase as 'homo currit', which can be taken to mean 'a man runs' or 'man runs'. Confused

---

[39] The discussion of these various kinds of supposition may be found in the *Tractatus*, ed. de Rijk, pp. 79-88; Mullaly, pp. 2-19. The further division of confused supposition into that which is confused by the requirements of the sign or of the thing (*necessitate signi sive rei*) is discarded at the end of the treatise on suppositions and therefore need not occupy us here.

supposition is the acceptance of a common term for many things by means of a universal sign, as in 'Every man is an animal'.

There are many more ramifications of the doctrine, e.g., the "pure or merely confused" supposition (*suppositio confusa tantum*) and "confused and distributive" (*confusa et distributiva*), which are not discussed in Peter of Spain's tract, but appear prominently in William of Sherwood, and with many modifications in Ockham.[41] Vives refers to these as well (he capitalizes on the latent humor of such expressions as '*confusa tantum*'), and these distinctions are crucial to the solving of some of the sophisms which he cites. Modern logicians recognize these experiments in the invention of terminology as a laudable achievement of the medieval logicians, which parallels certain modern developments of the science. It has been observed, for example, that in William of Sherwood's elaboration of the 'merely confused' supposition, there is recognition of the problem of multiple quantification and the extension of the scope of a quantifier to include another. In reality, the highly systematized, if somewhat barbarous, form of Latin which they devised was still inadequate for the exigencies of their science. Today, highly formal systems of symbols which employ one sign for one function, have almost replaced natural language altogether, thus eliminating the problem of determining the functions of equiform signs in each given instance, one of the tasks attempted by the theory of supposition. Their real accomplishment was to have brought to light weaknesses of the traditional Aristotelian logic in their effort to formulate some of its syntactical and semantical presuppositions.[42]

Vives returned to the discussion of logic and its place in the curriculum in a more positive vein in the third part of his *De disciplinis*, written in 1531. Here, in his own adaptation of the widely

---

[41] Cf. Kretzmann, *op. cit.*, pp. 117-121.

[42] An excellent, clear account of the medieval contribution to logic is given by Ernest A. Moody in *Studies in Medieval Philosophy, Science and Logic* (Berkeley, 1975), pp. 371-392. Cf. also the remarks of Walter Ong, *op. cit.*, p. 53 ". . . one cannot but be struck by the fact that the charges leveled against medieval logic by the humanists—its aridity, its difficulty, its finicky attention to detail, its highly technical vocabulary, its concern with real or apparent possibilities (*insolubilia, impossibilia, sophismata*), not to mention Ramus' celebrated charge that 'ordinary people don't talk like that'—are singularly like the charges often leveled against mathematical logic today."

disseminated teachings of the famous Frisian scholar, Rudolph Agricola, himself a product of the Italian schools,[43] Vives argued for a new kind of logic based on the art of invention and framed in a comprehensible, humane language. No longer should logic be considered a merely demonstrative science, equipping the student for endless verbal jousting, but it should serve as a guide, an *instrumentum*,[44] in all other studies. The parameter of discourse was to be enlarged from the vain syllogistic quibblings of scholastic language to more practical spheres of human activity.[45] This more humanistic approach to logic, uniting the separate disciplines of rhetoric and dialectic, with its emphasis on invention and disposition of argument, led to a much more generalized view of dialectic as simply the art of discoursing with probability on any subject,[46] as Ramus would later define it.

With his usual sense of moderation Vives does not presume to reject the Aristotelian framework, as Ramus does,[47] but he does voice some criticism of the *Categories* and the *Topics*. Most of his censure, however, is directed at the erroneous interpretations of Aristotle's teachings. As for the logicians' claim for the utility of their subject in sharpening the wits of the students, Vives counters that such mental agility could be gained just as well in reading

---

[43] Rudolph Agricola, or Roelof Huysman, introduced into Northern Europe ideas which he had imbibed at the *contubernium* of Ferrara with such scholars as Guarino Veronese and Theodore of Gaza. His *De inventione dialectica*, following closely on the heels of the successful dissemination of the writings of George of Trebizond, was in great vogue between the years 1515 and 1530. Vives incorporated many of Agricola's reforms in the art of rhetoric and dialectic into his *De tradendis disciplinis*. He would have probably been made familiar with the teachings of Agricola through the epitome of the *De inventione dialectica* published by Bartolomée Latomus, and the edition of the work by Martin Dorp.

[44] Majansius, VI, 146.

[45] In one passage of the *In pseudo-dialecticos*, Vives mockingly contrasts the vain science of the sophists, alien to all human activities, to the life of the artisans, who, if they were to understand what the holy doctors were saying, would rise up in force and drive them from the city. More insidious, however, was their corruption of the theological doctrines with their multiple distinctions and contorted terminology, making of theology "the exclusive monopoly of a clerical elite", as McConica remarks, *op. cit.*, p. 160.

[46] His simple definition of dialectic, as found in his *Dialecticae partitiones*, first published in 1543, is: 'Ars dialectica doctrina est disserendi'. Cf. Ong, *op. cit.*, p. 160.

[47] In his *Aristotelicae animadversiones*, first published in 1543. Successive editions of this work became more and more elaborate until they filled twenty books in 1548.

the classics. The restoration of the study of grammar and the classical authors to their rightful position in the curriculum is but the first step in the Spanish scholar's pedagogical reforms. During his stay at Oxford, he had experimented with his curricular innovations and helped in the establishment of the new studies there together with other illustrious teachers, such as Thomas Lupset and Nicholas Udall.

As Vives developed his educational ideas, however, he deviated more and more from the strict humanistic code of emulation of the classics, urging that we should not only build on the wisdom of the ancients but add to it. In the preface to the *De disciplinis* he argues that human nature is not deplete but full of new energy, capable of bringing forth new ideas. In support of his contentions he quotes a phrase of Seneca, "Qui ante nos ista moverunt, non domini nostri, sed duces sunt," ("Those who initiated such things before us are not our masters but our guides").[48] In contrast to the bookish learning of Erasmus, Vives' interests are more universal and concrete. He exhorts the student to be interested in all aspects of human activity, from the highest realms of spirituality and philosophy to the humbler world of husbandry and the practical arts of the artisan. Law, medicine, natural philosophy, architecture are included in his encyclopaedic outline of learning. The final end of such training should be moral excellence, combined with practical wisdom after the Platonic and Augustinian ideal. Knowledge is not something to be cultivated for its own sake but is to be translated into action. The ideal is far from the typical product of the Sorbonne, adept in screaming out his altercations, dazzling his adversary with a flurry of incomprehensible language and gaining the approval of the fans in the gallery.

The scope of Vives' teachings goes beyond the reform of the curriculum, for in the *De anima* in particular he had introduced some revolutionary ideas concerning what would now be called educational psychology. He was interested in the process of learning, psychosomatic relationships, the association of ideas as an aid to memory, even psychological conditioning as a phenomenon of memory. He saw the relevance of physiological features and individual temperaments in the problem of learning, here anticipating the ideas of Juan Huarte's *Examen de ingenios* and the Catalan

---

[48] Majansius, VI, 6-7.

school of the *sentit comun*. Indeed his teaching concerned itself with every aspect of the mechanism of human actions from inception in sense knowledge to final implementation in decisions of the will.

In the field of pedagogy Vives is the leading light of the sixteenth century, responsible for the empirical turn in its direction.[49] His influence can be detected in the works of the most famous pedagogical writers of the time—Roger Ascham, Richard Mulcaster, Johann Sturm and Comenius. His personal piety and austerity of life set him apart from the Italian humanists and from some of his Northern confreres, who occasionally gave signs of a furtive neo-paganism, and there can be no doubt that his Jewish origins were an obstacle to his career, as well as to his proper evaluation by posterity. It is time that he emerge from the shadow of more well-known contemporary figures to assume his rightful place in the history of ideas in fulfillment of his own motto, "Semper vivas."

---

[49] Cf. the fine article of Rita Guerlac, "Vives and the Education of Gargantua", *Etudes Rabelaisiennes* (Geneva, 1974), pp. 63-72.

JUAN LUIS VIVES

AGAINST THE PSEUDO-DIALECTICIANS

IOANNIS LVDOVICI VIVIS

IN PSEUDODIALECTICOS

AGAINST THE PSEUDO-LOGICIANS

My dear Fort,[1]

Since I thought that I should see you shortly in Paris, where I was planning to go from one day to the next, I expected to discuss these matters with you personally there. Unfortunately, since I cannot leave Louvain [2] because of my pursuits here, and thus do not know when I shall be able to see you, I am forced to commit my thoughts to a letter. In any case, I did not think that I should delay any further in acquainting you with the criticisms that I have heard from certain very learned friends of mine.[3] In our friendly conversations together, whenever reference is made to the rebirth of the humanities,[4] more particularly the origins of this revival, or to the state of the other higher disciplines, we cannot help feeling a certain pride in our age. On the other hand, these same scholars often complain that in Paris, the very citadel of learning, the center from which all new ideas should be radiated abroad, certain individuals have espoused a hideous form of barbarism, and are propagating outrageous doctrines or "soph-

---

[1] Juan Fuertes or Fort was a student in Paris under Juan Dolz of Aragon in 1511, as can be determined in references to him in various works of Dolz. He was a *contubernalis* of Vives, who introduces him as one of the speakers in the *Christi Jesu Triumphus*, an early work in the form of a dialogue which takes place in the poor quarters of their teacher, Gaspar Lax de Sariñena. An edition of Hyginus is also dedicated to Fort, and he is mentioned in the preface to Vives' lectures on the *Georgics*.

[2] At this time, following the sudden death of his young patron, Guillaume de Croy, Vives was constrained to make a livelihood lecturing at the University of Louvain.

[3] Numbered among these learned acquaintances were Erasmus himself, Adrian Dedel, rector of the university, and Martin Dorp, to mention only a few of the most prominent.

[4] In his letter of May, 1515 to Martin Dorp in rebuttal of certain charges made against the *Praise of Folly*, Erasmus alludes several times to the rebirth of good learning (*bonae litterae*) and the new life springing from it. The humanists were confident that this return to the classical authors would put an end to the tyranny exercised by the pedants and charlatans of the schools, and in its renewed attention to eloquence of style would usher

IOANNES LVDOVICUS VIVES
IOANNI FORTI SUO
S.D.

Quum existimarem futurum breui, mi Fortis, ut te Parisiis uiderem, quo ire quotidie constituebam, credebam etiam me haec eadem tecum coram acturum, quae (quoniam per occupationes meas non licet mihi Louanio egredi, neque sat scio, quando istuc ibo)
5 litteris sum modo necessario commissurus. Neque enim duxi diutius differendum, quo minus redderem te certiorem, quid iampridem expostulant mecum homines doctissimi, & amantissimi mei. Quibuscum familiariter dum commentor incidimusque in mentionem renascentium litterarum, & simul cum illis, hoc est, cum suo
10 seminario, disciplinarum omnium meliorum, id enim fere agimus, ut gratulemur nostro saeculo. Maxime queri illi solent Parisiis unde lux totius eruditionis manare deberet, mordicus homines quosdam foedam amplecti barbariem, & cum ea monstra quaedam disciplinarum, uelut sophismata, ut ipsi uocant, quibus nihil neque

---

Title: IOANNIS ... PSEUDODIALECTICOS] IOANNIS LO/DOVICI VIVIS / Valentini Opuscula uaria. / Meditationes in septem psalmos poenitentiae. / De tempore quo natus est CHRISTVS. / Clypei CHRISTI descriptio. / Triumphus CHRISTI IESV, / Ouatio Virginis dei parentis. / Veritas fucata. / Anima Senis. / De initiis Sectis & laudibus Philosophiae. / Fabula de Homine. / Praefatio in Georgica Vergilii. / Genethliacon IESV CHRISTI. / Praefatio in Leges Ciceronis. / Aedes Legum. / Pompeius fugiens. / In Pseudodialecticos. / Louanii in Aedibus Theodorici / Martini Alustensis; IOAN/NES LODOVICVS / Viues, Valentinus, aduersus / pseudodialecticos. / EIUSDEM POM/peius fugiens. / Selestadii apud Lazarum / Schurerium. / M.D.X.X. IOANNES ... S.D.) IOANNES LO/douicus Viues Ioanni Forti suo S.D. L; IOANNIS LO/DOVICVS VIVES IOANNI / forti suo S.D. S 1 Parisiis) Parrhisiis L S   2 quotidie] quottidie L
10 meliorum,] meliorum. L S   11 saeculo.] saeculo, L: saeculo; S   11 Parisiis] Parrhisiis L S   13 quosdam foedam] quosdam obscuram foedamque S   13 ea monstra] ea tenebras monstra S

---

in a new era of *humanitas*. Cf. *Letter to Martin Dorp*, 1515 trans. Betty Radice, accompanying the Penguin translation of the *Praise of Folly*, (Harmondsworth, 1971), p. 226.

isms",[5] as they refer to them, which are unrivalled in their vanity and stupidity. When men of genuine talent decide to dedicate themselves to such pursuits, their valuable mental abilities go to waste and like fertile fields left uncultivated, they produce a useless accumulation of weeds. Indulging in idle reveries, they devise nonsense for themselves and a new type of language which they alone can understand.

A great number of scholars lay the entire blame for this situation on the Spaniards resident there,[6] who, being men of unequalled abilities, have become energetic defenders of these bulwarks of ignorance, and since gifted intellects prevail wherever they are engaged, have come to excel in these insanities, if indeed one can speak of excellence in such a lowly and despicable pursuit. As a result, it is said that they render a grave disservice to the entire University of Paris, and are responsible for its infamous reputation among all nations. Who is not familiar with the current saying that in Paris our youth are taught nothing save to rant and rave in displays of endless verbosity? Other institutions have their useless and futile branches of learning, but much that is substantial as well, whereas only in Paris does one encounter the most idiotic and frivolous frothings to the exclusion of all else. It is suggested that the Spaniards of this persuasion together with all their disciples should be persuaded to turn their talents to other more worthy disciplines, or be expelled by public edict as corruptors of learning and morals. The French are truly determined to put an end to all this foolishness in one way or another. I, too, come in for censure

---

[5] From the study of linguistic subtleties required for the detection of fallacies and sophisms, the training in logic had gradually degenerated into a specialized science of sophistic for its own sake with the result that the terms logician and sophist were often used synonymously. Vives has some harsh words for his former colleagues at the beginning of the *De causis corruptarum artium*, comparing them to bilge water, where all foul substances collect (Majansius, VI, 130). In the very first treatise of the *Parva logicalia* Peter of Spain uses a sophism to illustrate his definition of indeterminate supposition. Indeed, one could say with de Rijk that the doctrine of fallacy forms the basis of terminist logic. Cf. L. M. de Rijk, *Logica modernorum* I (Assen, 1962), p. 22.

[6] In his letter to Erasmus of June 4th, in which he recounts his visit to Paris and the favorable reception of his tract against the logicians, Vives mentions some of the young Spaniards there who showed great promise. He names Juan Martin Poblacion, author of a treatise on the astrolabe,

uanius est, neque stultius. Quae cum exactius homines nonnulli
ingeniosi consectantur, tum sua bona ingenia perditum eunt, tum
tamquam fertiles agri sed inculti, magnam inutilium herbarum
procreant copiam. Somniant & confingunt sibi ineptias ac nouam
5 quandam linguam quam ipsi soli intelligant.

Pars maxima doctorum hominum totam huiusce rei culpam in
Hispanos, qui istic sunt reiicit, qui ut sunt homines inuicti, ita
fortiter tuentur arcem ignorantiae, & optima ingenia, ubi inten-
duntur, ualent, tradunt sese his deliramentis, fiunt in illis summi,
10 siquidem in re infima & despicatissima quisquam summus esse
potest. Ita eos pessime mereri aiunt de toto studio Parisiensi, ut
qui illud infame apud gentes omnes reddant. Quod enim est tam
tritum hominum sermone prouerbium, quam illud, Parisiis doceri
iuventutem nihil scire, atque adeo insane & loquacissime delirare?
15 Reliquis omnibus in studiis, etsi sunt uana & futilia nonnulla, esse
tamen solida multa, in unis Parisiis uix esse nisi nugacissimas nugas,
debere Hispanos eiusmodi simul cum aliis omnibus qui eos sectan-
tur, aut cogi ut aliis melioribus esse dederent disciplinis, aut edicto
publico expelli tamquam corruptores & morum & eruditionis.
20 Nam per Gallos non stare, quominus finis aliquando tandem fiat
desipiendi. Ita & me quoque increpant, qui pro mea parte uos,

---

2 ingenia preditum] ingenia corruptum & perditum S   3 inutilium] inuti-
liam V   9 deliramentis] delyramentis L S   18 aut] *om.* S   18 aut
edicto . . . eruditionis] *om.* S   21 qui] quis V

---

which he has occasion to praise elsewhere; Francisco de Mello, a gifted
mathematician, later appointed tutor to the King of Portugal's sons; a
Juan Enzinas, identified by Allen with Fernando de Enzinas of Valladolid,
author of several works on logic. Cf. Allen 1108, IV, p. 271. As for the
charge made against the Spaniards for their part in the propagation of
the Parisian doctrine, one must admit to a considerable representation of
Spanish authors in the plethora of terminist logic textbooks which came
streaming from Paris presses in the latter part of the 15th century. Cf.
Ricardo Villoslada, *La Universidad de Paris durante los estudios de Francisco
de Vitoria O. P.* (1507-1522), *Analecta Gregoriana* XIV (Rome 1938), pp.
51-53. Vives' own teacher, Gaspar Lax de Sariñena, was one of the most
prolific authors of such texts to emerge from the college of Montaigu, with
an impressive series of texts on exponibles, *insolubilia*, etc. to his credit.
(A complete list of his publications is given in Villoslada, *op. cit.*, pp. 405-406).
The principal stigma attaching to the Spanish name was, of course, ultimately
derived from the incalculable and in Vives' estimation, deleterious influence
of Peter of Spain.

for not doing what I can to suggest better things to those of you studying there. Do you think that I am unaffected by all this, my dear Fort? Not that I consider their accusations to be false, (for who will deny that such is the true state of affairs? you yourself are tacitly aware of it, and there is no need to mention names). But what disturbs me is that my fellow citizens and countrymen, whom through feelings of patriotic affection I should not like to hear spoken of save in the highest terms, should be held in such low regard. Moreover, I sense that part of this harsh criticism is applicable to me as well, since I was once one of their number, nor have I completely forgotten all those "asses",[7] and that pretentious vocabulary—*tantum, alter, alius, uterque, incipit, desinit, immediate.*[8] This is the principal reason for my entering upon this argument, for if I were not well-versed in the learning vaunted by these senseless individuals, I should not even presume to open my mouth against them, knowing that in their customary arrogance they would immediately retort, "He condemns what he does not understand."

But you can testify, as can others among my fellow students, that I had no mere smattering of these inanities, but might well be said to have acquired an intimate knowledge of them,[9] if one can speak in such terms of something which, in that it is a vice, becomes all the more dangerous when one refuses to recognize it as such. I do not say these things out of vainglory, for I can see no grounds for boasting. I wish I had never progressed so far in this nonsense, which took such root in my tender mind and youthful enthusiasm that I cannot rid myself of it. Even against my will it presents itself to my mind and obsesses my thoughts. I am made more aware of its detrimental effects when I turn to more worthwhile pursuits, for it often forces me to be trivial and foolish in very

---

[7] In scholastic examples the ass, and in particular Brunellus, was used very commonly to represent the realm of non-intelligent beings. It is interesting to note that there still exists in modern Spanish the verb *desasnar* (literally, to "de-ass"), meaning to instruct or civilize, which is put to good account in Jimenez' famous spiritual conversations with his ass, Platero.

[8] The "enigmatists" of the Parisian schools gave great currency to these syncategorematics, qualifying and conjunctive words that were used to modify and determine the terms of prepositions. A tract on *syncategoremata* is found appended to editions of Peter of Spain's *Summulae*, and is usually attributed to him. It follows directly on the seventh tract of that work,

qui istic estis, meliorum non admoneo. Parum putas, mi Fortis,
me plerumque hisce uerbis commotum? Non quod eos falsa dicere
crederem (quis enim rem ipsam ita se habere non uidet? Quam
ipse tacita tua cogitatione satis agnoscis, non est opus ut quenquam
5 nominem) sed quod ad eum modum de ciuibus deque conterraneis
meis existimarent, de quibus omnibus patria quadem charitate
nollem nisi quam optime ab omnibus & sentiri & praedicari. Tum
etiam quod ad me quoque partem illius uituperationis attinere
existimarem, qui aliquando ex isto numero fui, nec sunt mihi adhuc
10 asini omnes, & portentosa illa uocabula — tantum, alter, alius,
uterque, incipit, desinit, immediate — obliterata, quae una est atque
ea praecipua causa, quare de hac ista re loqui audeo. Nam si haec
quibus homines inepti gloriantur nota mihi non essent, ne hiscere
quidem in his auderem. Noui enim quid confestim solita sua
15 insolentia iactant: 'Damnat quia non intelligit.'

Verum tu es ipse testis, sunt & alii condiscipuli mei, me non
degustasse solum has insanias, sed etiam intima paene illarum
penetrasse, modo intimum esse possit in re, quae utpote uitium, in
immensum protenditur periculum si quis non credit. Non haec
20 gloriandi gratia dico, neque enim gloriae materiam ullam uideo.
Utinam non tam in illis promouissem, quae quoniam tenero adhuc
animo accepi, summoque cum studio, ideo tam tenaciter haerent,
ut elui nulla a me arte queant, & mihi uel inuito occurrant, ob-
uersenturque praesenti in cogitatione. Sentio quanto sint plerumque
25 impedimento, quum ad res meliores pergo, cogunt me interdum in

---

1 admoneo] admoneam S   14 auderem] deberem S   18 in] *om.* S   22
cum] *om.* S

---

which is known variously as the *de proprietatibus terminorum*, the *parva
logicalia*, or the *logica moderna*, and elaborates in greater detail the treatment
of these modifying words and expressions, which have special logical and
semantic effects on other terms in the proposition.
    [9] In recommending the young Vives as tutor for Cardinal de Croy, Erasmus
writes to Hermann, Count of Neuenahr, that as a student, Vives was invincible in sophistic debate, and that no one combined such skill in philosophy
with such a degree of eloquence (*tantum eloquentiae cum tanta philosophiae
cognitione*). Allen, 1082, p. 209. In a letter to Thomas More, written probably
sometime in June 1520, he is gratified to know that his learned colleague
shares his own esteem for Vives' abilities. He calls him a man of extraordinary philosophical genius (*animo mire philosophico*), and speaks of his
brilliant career in the sophists' own camp. Allen, 1107, p. 270.

serious matters. If there were teachers who could unteach these subjects, as there are those who teach them, I should seek them out with all haste and offer them a rich reward, as did the famous musician Timotheus.[10] I find myself in the same predicament as the Greek hero Themistocles, who is said to have replied to Simonides, a teacher of the art of memory: "I should rather forget than remember."[11] Similarly, I should be willing to pay as much to unlearn certain things as I would to learn others. If only one could exchange or give away these useless bits of knowledge, as one does with money, clothing, books, and other such possessions. There are those who spend much money to attain this learning, but I should pay them just as much to unburden me of what I know and take it for themselves. In this way they would be making a threefold profit, as they could immediately perceive; viz., the money saved, which they would have had to spend for the acquisition of this knowledge, the money that they would be receiving from me, and the gratuitous gift of this unlearned learning. I beseech you to consider not the possible merits of this science, but rather what keeps it from being publically repudiated as some sort of plague and corruption of sound minds.

In a letter to such a prudent man as yourself, I cannot and should not be prolix, and shall therefore confine myself to the main issues. I beg you and any others who read this not to be dismayed, but to bring your reasoning powers to bear and listen to my words with impartiality, reserving your judgement and opinions, expressed or tacit, until the end. The first thing we teach a boy in logic is that the study of logic is the road to the other disciplines.[12] But in what discipline does anyone in his right mind use such infelicities and senseless inanities as those illustrated in the following examples: 'only of any man whatever, besides Socrates, does any non-ass C whatever, and another C belonging to the same man, contingently begin to be black.' 'Angel non-A (whatever A and/or B is) ceases not to be angel.' And the result is no better when there is a sub-

---

[10] Timotheus was a poet and musician from Miletus (c. 450-c. 360 B.C.) who claimed to have revolutionized music in his free, astrophic compositions. The longest surviving examples of his poetry are portions of the *Persians*, extant in a papyrus of the fourth century B.C. The story is told in Quintilian, *Inst. Or.*, II, 3.3, that Timotheus charged a double fee for students who had studied previously with another master.

grauissimis ludere, atque ineptire. Et si quemadmodum magistri
sunt qui illa docent, ita essent qui dedocerent, ut Timotheus ille
musicus faciebat, ad hos ego me quam primum magna cum mercede
conferrem. Et sum modo in ea conditione, in qua olim princeps
5 Graeciae Themistocles, qui Simonidi artem memoriae tradenti
respondisse fertur, malle se obliuisci quam recordari, ita & sunt
mihi nonnulla quae tanti facerem dediscere, quanti alia addiscere
permulta. Utinam et pecuniam, uestes, libros, merces, & alia
huiusmodi, ita et haec commutare donareue liceret. Sunt qui magno
10 emunt haec scire, ego magno emerem ut his me illi exonerarent,
ut sibi acciperent. Ita facerent, ut ipsis quidem uideretur, triplex
emolumentum, & pecuniae quam daturi essent, & quam acciperent, & istius ineruditae eruditionis. Quae quid habeat dignum
propter quod, non dico ut amplexari debeat, sed ut ne reiici ab
15 omnibus publice tamquam pestis aliqua & ingeniorum corruptela
debeat, quaeso ipsi uos perpendite, & intra sese unusquisque ferat
sententiam.

Ego, & in epistola, & quae ad te tam prudentem uirum scribitur,
prolixus esse non possum, ac neque debeo, solum rei summas &
20 capita colligam. Te & alios, si qui sunt, qui haec legent, precor,
ne uos perturbatione aliqua rapi sinatis, sed aduocata in consilium
ratione, haec omnia aequis auribus et animo accipiatis, iudicium
sententiamque nec uoce nec tacita cogitatione ad finem usque
feratis. Hoc igitur primum docemus in dialectica puerum, esse
25 hanc uiam ad reliquas disciplinas, at qua in disciplina utitur quisquam sana mente istis tam insuauibus & fatuis ineptiis: 'Tantum
cuiuslibet hominis praeter Sortem quilibet non asinus c. & alterum
c, ipsiusmet hominis nigrum contingenter incipit esse. Desinit
Angelus, non a quodlibet a & b. Angelus non esse. 'Ne in illis

---

15 corruptela] *add.* non S   20 colligam] *add.* alias forsan de hac re per
otium copiosius & accuratius S   20 sunt qui] *om.* S   29 Angelus] *add.*
& angelus L S B

---

[11] The episode is recounted in Cicero, *De oratore*, II, 54. It is quoted also
in Castiglione's *Il cortegiano*, II, 1.

[12] "ad omnium methodorum principia viam habens", the definition of
dialectic par excellence, as enunciated at the very beginning of the *Sum-
mnlae*, was in the estimation of Professor Ong, the most repeated definition
in all scholastic philosophy. Walter J. Ong, *Ramus, Method, and the Decay
of Dialogue* (Cambridge, 1958), p. 56.

stitution of terms, as in: 'Any non-curate priesthood whatsoever with the exception of a canonry necessarily cannot be predicated solely of any priest whatsoever and any other priest.' [13] Who would deny that dialectic is a science of speech? This is made clear by its very name in Greek: *dialektike kai logike*,[14] corresponding to the pairing of rhetoric and grammar. Tell me, if you please, what language this logic of yours belongs to? French, Spanish, Gothic, or Vandal perhaps? It certainly is not Latin. The teacher of logic should use words and statements which will be intelligible to any-one who knows the language in which he is speaking, that is to say, Latin, if the logician professes to discourse in Latin; Greek, if in Greek. But these individuals, though claiming to speak Latin, not only are not understood by men versed in the Latin language, but often not even by men of the same flour, or should I say, husk.[15]

Many of their teachings are unknown to anyone save the one who devised them, and many more, strangely obscured and convoluted like the oracles of Apollo, require an explicator or interpreter en-dowed with divine intelligence. Or to use another paragon, almost everything that is treated in syllogisms, oppositions, conjunctions, disjunctions and explications are just like the riddles which children and gossiping women invent to amuse one another, for instance: "What is it that falls from above without breaking, but if it falls into the water, dissolves?", which reminds me of their favorite phrase: "Cite an instance." Is there any difference between the preceding example and the following: 'What is it that is of man any ass whatsoever but is not any ass whatsoever of man?' If you were to guess what lies concealed beneath these verbal wrappings, your interlocutor would have nothing more to respond, as in the case

---

[13] Although, strictly speaking, we cannot relegate these monstrous lucubrations of the logicians to the realm of *insolubilia*, (for the specific meaning of this term, cf. Paul Vincent Spade, "The Origins of Medieval Insolubilia Literature", *Franciscan Studies* 1973 pp. 292-309), these illustra-tions are for all practical purposes insoluble. Vives merely wishes to show how the Latin language was strained to the breaking point by the Parisian doctors so as to become unrecognizable to any speaker of the language. The first and third sentences are variations of the same form and modality, differing only in the terms to be substituted. The C of the first proposition is presumably to be replaced by a common term of the category of non-ass; e.g., "camel". As Vives clearly demonstrates, nothing is to be gained by the substitution of more specific verbal formulas for the simple syllogistic

quidem uocabulis quae quidam pro his substituunt: 'Tantum
cuiuslibet presbyteri & alius alterius presbyteri quodlibet sacer-
dotium non curatum praeter quam canonicatus necessario non est.'
Tum dialecticam quis non uidet scientiam esse de sermone? Quod
5 ostendit ipsa graeca nominis ratio, διαλεκτική καὶ λογική, uti est
rhetorice, uti & grammatice. Iam de quo, quaeso, sermone est
ista uestra dialectica? De gallicone an de hispano? an de gothico?
an de vandalico? Nam de latino certe non est. Dialecticus enim
iis ubi debet uerbis, iis enuntiationibus, quas nemo non intelligat,
10 qui sciat linguam illam, qua is loquitur, uelut latinam, si latine se
dialecticus profitetur disserere, graecam, si graece. At isti non dico
non intelliguntur a doctissimis latine, cum se latine dicant loqui,
sed interdum ne ab hominibus quidem eiusdem farinae, seu eiusdem
potius furfuris.

15 Sunt enim pleraque, quae nosse nemo potest, nisi is qui confinxit,
multa, quae tamquam Apollinis oracula mire contecta et conuoluta,
explicatore aliquo & interprete diuinae mentis egent. Tunc omnia
fere, quae in syllogismis, in oppositionibus, in coniunctionibus,
disiunctionibus, explicationibusque enuntiationem tractantur, aliud
20 non sunt, nisi quaestiones illae diuinandi, quas sibi inuicem pueri
& mulierculae inter lusus proponunt: 'Quae res est, quae ex alto
decidens non rumpitur, in aquam si ceciderit, dissoluitur'. Simile
prorsus est illud, quod isti semper habent in ore, 'Da casum'. Quid
enim aliud id sibi uult nisi, dic mihi: 'Quae res est, quae est hominis
25 quilibet asinus, non tamen est quilibet asinus hominis?' Quos si
tu diuinaris, quid illud sit, quod sub illis uerborum inuolucris
contectum latet, quid alter mutire possit, non habet, ut ille, qui

---

letter names. The negative-laden sentence about angels is probably meant
to illustrate that the useless accumulation of negatives results finally in an
affirmative statement, viz., that an angel does not cease to be angel, even
when designated by a negative term, non-A. As for the interpretation of
these puzzles, one must agree with Vives that they would require the interven-
tion of the Delphic oracle.

14 The Greek word *dialektike* is, of course, related to the word *dialektos*,
which meant both "speech" or "language" in general, as well as the specific
language or dialect of a given region.

15 The play on words is difficult to reproduce, for it depends on a late
Latin idiom, in which *homo eiusdem farinae* has the meaning of "a man of the
same ilk or paste" to use the closest English equivalents. Vives substitutes
for *farina* the alliterative *furfur*, "bran", the coarse part of the grain, which
was proverbially accounted as useless.

of the man who proposed as a riddle: "What is it that is earth-born, slow of foot, house-carrying and bloodless?" When the answer was given that it was a snail, he lapsed into silence, for there was nothing more that he could add to his question. Fortunately, their discussions are carried on in some form of the Latin language, no matter how bad or corrupt it may be, for if such madness were understood by the common people, the whole working-class to a man would drive them out of the city with hisses, shouts and the clanging of the tools of their trade. Such would be a fitting punishment for these fools, who lack any degree of common sense. Is anyone of the opinion that Aristotle fitted his logic to a language which he had invented for himself, instead of to the current form of Greek which everyone spoke?

Their logic is truly something extraordinary, expressed in a language which they claim to be Latin, but which Cicero, if he were to come back to life, would not understand. It is just as much a defect in logic as it would be in grammar or rhetoric for someone to use a language that he has invented himself instead of that used by the rest of mankind. These three arts deal with language [16] which came from the people and not from teachers, for first the Latin and Greek languages existed, and afterwards grammatical, rhetorical and logical formulas were observed in them. Language was not twisted to suit the rules, but rather the rules followed the pattern of the language. We do not speak Latin in a certain way because Latin grammar bids us so to speak; on the contrary, grammar recommends us to speak in a certain way because that is the way Latin is spoken. The same is true of rhetoric and logic, each of which is expressed in the same language as grammar. That is how we determine the truth or falsehood of a statement. Logic finds out truth, falsehood, or probability in the common speech that everyone uses, as rhetoric discovers ornament, brilliance, or gracefulness of expression. Whoever is ignorant of this fact is indeed abysmally ignorant, and runs aground in the harbor, or like the gelding of Sulpicius Galba,[17] falls down at the

---

[16] Logic, like the other two subjects of the medieval trivium, was considered a *scientia sermocinalis*, i.e., having to do with language, but in the eyes of the humanists it had been corrupted by the professional logicians into a kind of non-language.

cum proposuisset, 'quid esset terrigena, tardigrada, domiporta, sanguine cassa', dictumque ei fuisset esse cochleam, obticuit. Neque enim aliquid illi erat quod adiicere suae quaestioni ualeret. Quare praeclare agitur cum istis hominibus, quod disputant, licet cor-
5 ruptissime, licet pessime, aliqua tamen specie sermonis latini. Nam si a uulgo tales dementiae intelligerentur, tota opificum turba illos e ciuitate supploderet, sibilis, clamoribus, strepituque suorum instrumentorum eiiceret, tamquam stupidos quosdam homines, & carentes sensu communi, quales sunt omnes fere, qui istis in
10 rebus uersantur. An putat quispiam Aristotelem suam dialecticam ad sermonem, quem ipse sibi confinxerat, & non potius ad uulgarem illum Graecum, quem totus populus loquebatur, accommodasse?

Mira profecto istorum dialectica, cuius sermonem, quem ipsi latinum esse uolunt, Cicero, si nunc resurgeret, non intelligeret.
15 Quod non minus profecto uitium in dialectica est, quam si in gram-matica, si in rhetorica, sermone quisquam utatur, quem ipse sit commentus, non quo ceteri homines utantur. Sunt enim hae tres artes de sermone, quem a populo accipiunt, non ipsae tradunt. Nam prius fuit sermo latinus, prius graecus, deinde in his formulae
20 grammaticae, formulae rhetoricae, formulae dialectices obseruatae sunt, nec ad illas detortus est sermo, sed illae potius sermonem sunt secutae, & ad eum sese accommodarunt. Neque enim loquimur ad hunc modum latine, quia grammatica latina ita iubet loqui, quin potius e contrario, ita iubet grammatica loqui, quoniam sic Latini
25 loquuntur. Res eodem modo se habet in rhetorice & dialectice, quarum utraque in eodem sermone uersatur, quo grammatica. Unde est illud uerum & falsum praesupponere congruum. Dialectica itaque in hoc uulgari, & qui est omnium in ore sermo, uerum, falsum, probabilitatem inuenit, rhetorice uero ornatum, splendorem,
30 gratiam. Quae qui ignorat, is profecto imperitissimus est, & in portu impingit, ac uelut cantherius ille Sulpitii Galbae, longum

---

3 illi] ei S   3 ualeret] posset S   8 eiiceret] *add.* & propelleret S   17 quo ceteri homines] qui ceteris hominibus communis sit S   18 non ipsae] ipsae non S   22 sunt secutae] secutae sunt S

---

[17] The story is told that Sulpicius Galba's nag collapsed as he was setting out for the provinces. Cf. Sextus Pompeius Festus, *De verborum significatu: quae supersunt, cum Pauli Epitome* (Leipzig, 1913) p. 356. In proverbial usage the anecdote refers to those who are exhausted before they ever begin.

gate before ever getting started on his journey. Similarly, if one goes astray at the beginning of one's education, it is inevitable that the more he progresses, the farther he will stray. If there is still someone too hardheaded to admit this in words or in thought, I advise him, whoever he may be, to take ship without delay and set sail for Anticyra to free his brain from madness with a draught of hellebore.[18]

Yet I am astonished to think that anyone could not understand this, if he were to reflect for a moment on the procedure of these arts. For in grammar, "homo est albus" is not a Latin sentence because grammar so rules, and in rhetoric figures of speech do not lend brilliance and polish to elocution because rhetoric so prescribes, but rather because the Roman people, who spoke true Latin, judged that sentence to be Latin. Accordingly, the grammarian does not prescribe that it is Latin, but he teaches that it is; and since certain figures of speech seemed beautiful and ornamental to the speakers, the art of rhetoric has carefully transmitted these observations. In the same way, in logic it is usage that ultimately determines whether a certain statement in the indicative mood is true or false, or another statement in another mood is not true or false. Logic does not declare that 'Man is an animal and an animal is a body' is a conjunctive statement while 'You are white or you are black' is a disjunctive statement, and automatically so it must be. For before logic was ever discovered, these rules taught by the logician were already in existence; he merely transmits them, because the consensus of speakers, whether of Latin or of Greek, so sanctions. Consequently, the precepts of logic no less than those of grammar or rhetoric were adapted to the common usages of speech. But these so-called sophists must compensate in some way for their lack of talent and learning, which prevents them from attaining a reasonable success in debate and argumentation with the stock vocabulary available to everyone from a common public coinage. Forgetful of the true function of the logician, which is the skillful manipulation of ordinary vocabulary, they have invented private meanings for words contrary to the customs and conventions of mankind, so

---

[18] Hellebore, a pungent medicinal plant that grew in the neighborhood of Anticyra, a port of Phocis at the head of the gulf of Corinth, was supposed, in classical times, to be a cure for madness. There were two varieties of

ingressus iter, in porta cadit, quumque in exordio suae disciplinae
fallatur, necesse est ab illa eo longius aberret, quo magis promouerit.
Quod si quisquam fuerit, qui haec pertinaciter & uerbis & animo
pernegarit, huic ego consulo, quisquis tandem fuerit, ut ne horulam
5 ac ne momentum quidem moretur, quo minus quamprimum nauim
conscendat, & ad cerebrum helleboro ab insania liberandum, recta
nauiget Anticyras.

Quamuis miror aliquem esse, qui haec ignorare possit, modo
paululum cogitationi de harum artium ratione uelit intendere.
10 Nam ut in grammatica, non idcirco haec est latina oratio, 'Homo
est albus,' quod illa sic praecipit, nec in rhetorica schemata illa
eloquutioni nitorem & cultum afferunt, quod rhetorica iubet, sed
potius quod illam orationem populus Romanus, qui uere latine
loquutus est, latinam iudicauit. Ideo grammaticus non iubet eam
15 esse latinam, sed docet, & quia pulchra illustriaque uidebantur
illa schemata loquentibus, idcirco rhetorica diligentia ea obseruata
tradidit. Ad eundem modum in dialectica usu uenit. Non enim
quia praecipit ipsa enuntiationem eam esse ueram uel falsam, quae
est de indicatiuo, eam non esse, quae est de aliis modis, continuo
20 ita est, nec quia uult hanc esse coniunctionem siue coniunctiuam,
'Homo est animal, & animal est corpus,' aut hanc esse disiunctiuam.
'Tu es albus, uel tu es niger,' protinus & ita res habet. Nam antequam ulla dialectica inueniretur, ea erant, ut dialecticus esse docet,
quae idcirco docet, quoniam loquentium siue latine siue graece
25 consensus approbat, quapropter praecepta dialectices non minus,
quam grammatices atque rhetorices ad usum loquendi communem
aptanda sunt. Verum isti qui sophistae nominantur, quoniam
ingenium eis deerat, & eruditio, qua quiduis auditori & contra
disputanti uerisimiliter probare possent, idque uulgaribus notisque
30 uocabulis atque orationibus, quibus unusquisque uti debet tamquam
nummis quibus publica forma est, quod erat uerum dialectici munus,
confinxerunt ipsi sibi nescio quos uocabulorum significatus contra

---

20 coniunctiuam] coniunctam S   31 munus, confinxerunt ipsi] munus,
idcirco ipsi S

---

the plant, black and white, which were often mixed with another local shrub
called sesamoides. The resulting concoction seems to have been quite potent.
Cf. Strabo IX, 418; Pliny, *Nat. Hist.*, XXV, 27.

that they may give the appearance of victory in debate by making themselves incomprehensible.

When they are understood, their stupid and insane methods become plain to everyone. Thus when they have a disputant so confused with their strange, unusual forms and structures of words, their mysterious suppositions,[19] amplifications, restrictions, and appellations, they declare themselves victors over an enemy left more befuddled than vanquished by the novelty of their verbal prestidigitations. Is there a Cato, Laelius, Cicero, Caesar, Sallust, Livy, Quintilian, Pliny or Marcus Varro [20] (who is said to have been the first to write in Latin on the subject of logic), who would not stop dead in his tracks in the face of statements like the following:[21]

> A drunken person (one of our logicians, no doubt) can swear by a stone image of Jupiter that he did not drink wine, because he did not drink the wine that is in India.

> The king of France, surrounded by a troupe of servants, really does not have servants, because the servants of the king of Spain do not belong to him.

> Varro, though a man, is likewise not a man because Varro is not Cicero.

> A head, no one has but it is also true that there is no man who is without a head.[22]

---

[19] For a summary treatment of the concept of supposition, the reader is referred to the introduction, pp. 11-15. Ampliation is defined by Peter of Spain as the extension of a common term from a narrower supposition to a wider, while restriction is the opposite process. Appellation is a kind of supposition that can be used only for existent, not simply hypothetical, beings. More detailed discussion of this aspect of medieval philosophy may be found in I. M. Bochenski, *A History of Formal Logic* (Notre Dame, 1961) pp. 173-175 and William and Martha Kneale, *The Development of Logic* (Oxford, 1962), pp. 246-265.

[20] The classical Latin writers here evoked are the usual authorities cited by the humanists as paragons of the best Latinity: Cato the Elder, who personified the laconic, pristine Latin style of oratory; Gaius Laelius, judged by later generations as one of the ablest orators of his day, a central figure in several of Cicero's dialogues; Julius Caesar, known for the purity and elegance of his style and second only to Cicero as an orator; Sallust, the historian, advocate of a very concise, antithetical type of discourse; Livy, esteemed for the richness and versatility of his language; Quintilian, author of the very influential treatise on the training of the orator, much admired in the Renaissance, especially by Vives and Erasmus in their pedagogical writings; Pliny the Younger, elegant stylist in his consciously litterary

omnem hominum consuetudinem & usum ut tunc uicisse uideantur,
cum non intelliguntur.

Nam cum intelliguntur, tunc plane nihil frigidius, nihil dementius
fieri posse omnes uident. Ita turbato eo, quicum certant, mira &
5 insinuata uocabulorum forma atque ratione, miris suppositionibus,
miris ampliationibus, restrictionibus, appellationibus, ipsi tunc sibi
ipsis nullo publico consilio atque sententia decernunt triumphum
de hoste nouis uerborum praestigiis turbato, non uicto. Etenim
quis Cato, Laelius, Cicero, Caesar, Sallustius, Livius, Quintilianus,
10 Plinius, & qui primus de dialectica scripsisse latine fertur, M. Varro,
non haereat, si quis istorum cum sit ebrius, Iouem lapideum iuret
se uinum non bibisse, quia uinum quod est in India, non biberit?
si cum uideat regem Galliae maxima famulorum manu stipatum,
alter aiat, regem hunc famulos non habere, quia non eius sint illi,
15 qui regi Hispaniae famulantur? Tum etiam si asserat, Varronem
cum sit homo, hominem tamen non esse, quia Cicero non ipse sit
Varro; caput nullum hominem habere, cum tamen nullus homo

---

1 usum,] usum confinxerunt, S   5 forma] facie S   14 aiat] affirmet S
17 nullus] *add*. non 1520

---

letters; Marcus Terentius Varro, encyclopaedic writer of the first century
B.C., author of a treatise on the Latin language.

21 Most of the sophisms which Vives provides as examples of the bizarre
statements that were debated and expounded by the logicians are either
taken directly from the classroom or are closely modeled on those actually
in use, as may be verified in surviving lists of examples. From his own
training in these absurdities he is well-qualified to parody the inane quibbling
that delights in suppression of terms and semantic ambivalence.

22 The first four sophisms play on the subtle distinctions inherent in
the various kinds of personal supposition. The drunken logician of the
first sophistic conclusion would have reasoned something like this: 'I did
not drink the wine in India' which would be the *casus*. He can then continue:
'(Some) wine I did not drink.' The some in parentheses would not be in
the original Latin phrase, but could be conveniently inferred in the absence
of an initial quantifying word. Using more scientific language, one could
say that an indefinite proposition is sometimes equivalent for syllogistic
purposes to a particular proposition. In such a proposition the subject
term (not grammatical subject, but logical subject) is in determinate supposition, one of the varieties of personal supposition. From the statement
'Some wine I did not drink' one may validly descend to a series of disjuncts:
'The wine in India I did not drink, or the wine in Spain I did not drink,
etc.' The long disjunction will be true as a whole, although not all of the

There are more non-Romans than Romans in this room, in which there are a thousand Romans and two Spaniards.[23]

All the men in the world are non-seeing because there are some men who are blind.[24]

Any man's ass an animal is not, and is not an animal, not even an ass, and yet no one has ever seen an ass that is not both animal and ass.[25]

A harlot who has prostituted herself for many years in a whore-house will be a virgin, and conversely, the most chaste of virgins was for a long time a harlot and prostitute.[26]

Pepper is not sold in Paris and Rome, yet it is likewise true that in Paris or Rome no one can get pepper for nothing, but must buy it with good money, carefully counted and weighed out.[27]

Socrates, shut up in his prison, seeing one certain star sees every star, and yet does not see every star.[28]

---

single disjuncts will be true. The next logical (or illogical) inference would be that from '(Some) wine I did not drink' one could validly say 'I did not drink (some) wine.' With proper nouns, which have discrete supposition, the inference may be made, but the analogy does not hold for common nouns. In the statement '(Some) wine I did not drink; therefore, I did not drink (some) wine' the term wine has determinate supposition in the premise, but confused and distributive supposition in the conclusion. Thus the principle illustrated by the sophism is that one cannot make an inference from a sentence in which a term occurs in determinate supposition to a sentence in which it appears in confused and distributive supposition. The next example is based on exactly the same kind of confusion of supposition. One may not validly infer: '(Some) servants the king of France does not have; therefore the king of France does not have (some) servants.' Similarly, with the third and fourth examples: 'Varro is not Cicero' hence 'a or some man Varro is not.' While one may infer: 'Varro Cicero is not; therefore Varro is not Cicero', it does not follow that '(A, some) man Varro is not; therefore, Varro is not (a, some) man'. The case of no man with a head goes something like this: 'This head (the head of a goat for example) no man has; therefore, no man has the head of a goat.' Likewise: '(Some, a) head no man has; therefore, no man has a head.'

[23] The non-Romans may well denote *everything* other than Romans in the room, including the tiles in the floor, the shoes on their feet, etc.

[24] The equivocation in this example stems from the interpretation of the universal quantifier *omnes* in initial position. If some men are non-seeing (blind) then all men aren't seeing, and if all men aren't seeing, then all men are non-seeing. The ambiguity disappears in speech when one puts verbal emphasis on *all* as: '*All* men aren't Greeks' but the sophism relies on the written form of the statement.

capite careat; plures esse non Romanos quam Romanos in hac
aula, in qua sunt Romani mille, Hispani duo; omnesque homines,
qui sunt in orbe esse non uidentes, quia sunt caeci nonnulli; cuiusuis
hominis asinum & animal non esse, & non esse animal, ne asinum
5 quidem, quum adhuc nullus sit uisus asinus qui non sit & animal
& asinus. Si dicat quoque meretricem in lupanari multis prostratam
annis uirginem fore, & e diuerso, uirginem castissimam iamdiu
prostrasse, & scortum fuisse; & non uendi piper Parisiis &
Romae quum nec Parisiis, nec Romae piper gratis quisquam acci-
10 piat, sed bona bene numerata & bene appensa pecunia emat;
Socratem quoque in carcere clausum, unumque aliquod sidus
uidentem, uidere omne sidus, quum non omne sidus uideat; & hoc
axioma, siue ut Cicero transfert, pronuntiatum, esse uerum:

---

1 Romanos] Romani (bis) V   5 non] *om.* S   8 scortum] scorteum V
12 quum] quo S   13 pronuntiatum] *add.* ut Varro profatum ut Lelius
prologum S

---

25 Once again the moving of common terms across negation words leads to
logical confusion. 'Any man's ass (i.e. Socrates' ass, Plato's ass, etc.) Leo
the lion is not; therefore, any man's ass is not Leo the lion', but the analogy
does not hold when common terms are used.

26 This same obscure example is also cited in More's letter to Dorp, *Sir
Thomas More Selected Letters*, ed. Elizabeth Frances Rogers (New Haven,
1961) p. 22. Technically it is called the *fallacia secundum diversum tempus*.

27 The word pepper constituted a unique problem in the analysis of the
properties of terms. It could not be considered personal supposition, for
that would require in the appropriate kind of descent to singulars that
some one individual pepper was sold in both Paris and Rome, which is not
so. Thus it appears that the term stands for the species, and hence is in
simple supposition, but that is not true either, for no one buys or sells
a species in Paris or Rome or anywhere else. William of Sherwood tried to
introduce subdivisions of simple supposition to account for this. "Pepper
here supposits for its significatum as related in a general, unfixed way
to the things belonging to it. Thus it is often said that this is unfixed (*vaga*)
supposition." William of Sherwood, *Introduction to Logic* trans. Norman
Kretzmann (Minneapolis, 1966), p. 112.

28 There were many sophisms about Socrates the astronomer or the star-
gazer. In an example from Buridan's list of *sophismata*, Socrates, locked
up in a windowless jail and ignorant of what time it is, knows that some
stars are above, and yet there are no stars which he knows to be above. In
the Vives variation, he sees all stars that are to be seen and thus sees every
star.

The axiom [29] (or statement, as Cicero translates it), "Every man-who-has-a-son is a father," is true, while on the other hand "Every man is a father-who-has-a-son" is false.[30]

Socrates and this ass are brothers.[31]

Two contradictory statements despite their contradictory meanings are still true.[32]

In short, no one could remain so undaunted and undismayed in the face of these monstrous apparitions as not to implore the aid of Hercules, the legendary monster-killer.

I shall pass over propositions that are even more ludicrous for their utter fatuousness:

"Anti-Christ and the Chimaera are brothers." [33]
"Nothing and No-man bite each other in a sack." [34]
"The ass of Anti-Christ is the son of the Chimaera." [35]

At least these previous statements are written in a recognizable form of Latin, but the next batch, I dare say, would never be recognized as such by any inhabitant of the Latin world, ancient or modern:

"Every two opostles of God and another two apostles of God are twelve."[36]
',All all apostles of God are in this room."
"No non-man does not possibly not run." [37]

To all these negations, heaped one upon the other, crushed and stuffed together like dried figs or raisins in a basket, they add these no less egregious examples:

---

[29] Cicero translates the Greek logical term *axioma* as *pronuntiatum*, i.e., proposition, *Tusculan Disputations*, 1.7, 14: cf. also *Academica*, 29, 95.

[30] The position of relative clauses determines the truth or falsity of this statement. The first sentence is true, and is to be read: 'Every man-who-has-a-son is a father.' The second is false: 'Every man is a father-who-has-a-son.'

[31] Socrates, the medieval examplar of *homo sapiens*, is forever being contrasted with his non-intelligent cousin, the ass. In a far-fetched syllogism to be found in Buridan he becomes the son of an ass, the veracity of which depends on the implausible circumstance that one day he saw his father coming toward him in ass' (rather than sheep's) clothing, and thinking his father was an ass, became the son of an ass. Here, I suppose, the sophism depends on some such antecedent as the ass is a brother (to another ass) and Socrates (to another man), and therefore they are both brothers.

[32] With this paradigm Vives seems to be summing up those that preceded, showing that the medieval logicians, like the Sophists of old, could prove the same statement true or false by turns.

[33] Using the classical rhetorical figure of *praeteritio*, Vives goes on to mention a few more outlandish examples, all dependent upon the fallacious

'Omnis homo qui filium habet est pater,' quum hoc sit falsum:
'Omnis homo est pater, qui filium habet;' Socratem & hunc asinum
esse fratres; duas enuntiationes contradictorias, etiam in sensu
contradictorio ueras esse. Ita ut nemo sit tam imperterritus &
5 confidens, qui quum uideat haec monstra, non ilico Herculis illius
monstrorum depulsoris opem cogatur implorare.

Transeo illa, quae magis ad risum faciunt ex sua tanta fatuitate:
'Antichristus & Chimaera aunt fratres;' 'nihil et nemo mordent se
in sacco;' 'Asinus Antichristi est filius Chimaerae.' Atque haec
10 quidem uiderent utcumque latine esse dicta. Illa uero ausim deierare
in toto Latio, & antiquo & nouo, neminem unquam fuisse, qui
latina esse putasset: 'Omnes duo Apostoli Dei, & alii duo Apostoli
Dei sunt duodecim;' 'omnes omnes Apostoli Dei sunt in hac aula;'
'non non homo non possibiliter non currit;' negationibus aliis
15 super alias in pronuntiato inculcatis & infartis, tamquam in
cophino caricis aut uuis passis. Tum accedunt haec non minus

---

4 tam imperterritus] tam praesenti animo, tam confidens S   7 fatuitate]
fatuitate & insulsitate S

---

use of nothing and no-one as syllogistic terms. This first example may thus
be reconstructed: Anti-christ is the brother of no-one (in that he does not
yet exist), and no-one is the brother of the Chimaera (another hypothetical
figure). Hence Anti-christ is a brother of a brother of the Chimaera, and
consequently, Anti-christ and the Chimaera are brothers. The phoenix and
the unicorn were other favorite exemplars of non-beings.

[34] In the next one, let us suppose that the sack is empty, save for Plato
and Socrates, who are biting one another. Then, on the one hand, everything
in the sack is biting someone, so that there is nothing in the sack that is
biting no one. On the other hand, everyone in the sack is biting something,
so that no one in the sack is biting nothing. Therefore, nothing is biting
no one in the sack, and no one is biting nothing.

[35] The third of this ludicrous series is like the first: Nothing is the ass
of Anti-christ, but likewise, nothing is the son of the Chimaera. Hence,
the same thing is both the ass of Anti-christ and the son of the Chimaera.

[36] The twelve apostles were often conscripted to illustrate the peculiar
logical behavior of numerals and plural nouns. The basic riddle seems to be:
All the apostles are twelve. Peter and John are apostles. Therefore, Peter
and John are twelve. The sophism is given in this form in Heytesbury's
list of *sophismata*, where the distinction is explained as depending on the
interpretation of the term *'omnes'* either in a composite or divisive sense
(*'collective aut divisive'*). Curtis Wilson, *William Heytesbury, Medieval
Logic and the Rise of Mathematical Physics* (Madison, 1956) p. 159.

[37] Vives reprimands the logicians several times in the treatise for their
manipulation of negatives in defiance of the grammatical rules of the Latin
language. In this instance one could read *non non homo* either as 'no non-
man' or a 'non non-man (i.e. some man'). The four negatives of the sentence
ultimately cancel each other out.

"Anything of any kind knows of any such thing that it is such as it is." [38]

"Of the same man any ass is not both an ass and a non-ass." [39]

"Any man is every man." [40]

"Only a man and another second man are G."

"Any ass belonging to a man belongs to that same man and A."

"Of Sortes and the other F, the matter of the same F and any other man are."

"Any man not except non-Sortes does not run."

"Sortes not inasmuch as he is not a man, is not an animal."

And what of these?

"Of man C, as it were, any ass is the non-animal B."

"Man A and any non-Sortes of any kind are each necessarily the other man and D. P."

The use of A, B, C, and D determines whether these suppositions are confused, determinate, or mixed.[41] Add to the above sample even greater admixtures beyond the powers of a pharmacologist— E, F, G, H, I, and K—for some of them reach the twenty-first letter of the alphabet a second time through, mixing and jumbling weird suppositions of every sort in their wild hallucinations. Obviously they became envious of the lot of the mathematician, because he seemed to have a sole monopoly on the letters of the alphabet. As a result they took over the whole alphabet for their own use, so that no one could ever deny that they were extremely "literate." But when they proceed to mathematics, if God so grants them, they encounter difficulties, because they do not quite know what all those letters mean.[42] I hear that one of them

---

[38] Relying on the expertise of my logician informant in this very technical construct, I shall attempt a layman's explanation as follows: 'Choose anything x of any kind k. Then, for anything y, also of kind k, x knows of y that it is such as it is, viz., that it is of kind k.' From more modern examples, one may illustrate by citing that the police know that every criminal is a criminal, but it is not the case that every criminal is such that the police know that *he* is a criminal. This sophism is discussed in Peter of Spain *Summae Logicales*, ed. de Rijk, p. 13. The distributive sign *quilibet* is also discussed in this same context in William of Sherwood's *Treatise on Syncategorematic Words*, ed. Kretzmann (Minneapolis, 1968) p. 46: "Suppose that there are only the three qualities—(whiteness, literacy, music)—and that Socrates has them all and Plato likewise, and Cicero likewise, and that each of them knows this of the others. Suppose further that Virgil has only whiteness and that he knows nothing of the others nor they of him. Then everything of every sort knows of every such thing that it is such."

[39] The point here is once again the ambiguity of negatives. The Latin can be read as the trivial truth: 'any ass (the genitive modifier is unessential)

egregia: "Quodlibet qualelibet de quolibet tali scit ipsum esse tale,
quale ipsum est; ipsiusmet hominis quilibet asinus, non asinus &
non asinus est; ipsemet homo est quilibet homo; tantum homo &
alter alius homo sunt g; ipsiusmet hominis & a. quilibet asinus
5 hominis est; sortis & alterius f. materia ipsiusmet f. & quilibet
homo sunt; quilibet homo non praeter non Sortem non currit;
Sortes non inquantum non homo non est animal.' Quid illa? 'c.
hominis quasi quilibet asinus est b. non animal, a. homo & quilibet
qualislibet non Sortes uterque alter homo & d.p. necessario sunt;'
10 ut a.b.c.d. faciant illas suppositiones confusas, determinatas, & ex
his mistas. Adde etiam commistiones maiores, quam ullus unquam
pharmacopola facit, e.f.g.h.i.k., ita ut nonnulli ad decimam usque
litteram secundi alphabeti iam recurrerint, mira suppositionum
genera somniantes & confundentes. Inuiderunt scilicet isti homines
15 mathematicis, quod illi soli litteris uti uiderentur. Ideo & ipsi
quoque totum alphabetum suos in usus transtulerunt, ut nemo sit
cum haec uideat, qui possit negare eiusmodi homines esse litteratis-
simos. Verum cum ad mathematica pergunt, si hoc unquam deus
illis tribuit, offenduntur nonnihil, quod quid sibi elementa illi
20 uelint, parum sciunt. Audio quendam ex his, cum sese geometriae

---

1 egregia] lepida S   7 illa] *add.* de quolibet a. & cuiuslibet non b. asinum
non c. tantum d. praeter b. contingenter esse possible est & c, hominis quasi
quilibet asinus est b, non animal, a. homo S

---

is not both an ass and a non-ass', or as the falsehood: 'is a non-ass and a
non-ass'.

40 The rest of these examples are so fragmentary and cryptic that they
defy understanding, either in the original barbarous Latin or more barbarous English. Suffice it to say that Vives has made his point, and merely
hammers it home is a spurt of utter nonsense.

41 Peter of Spain distinguishes between determinate and confused supposition, and subdivides the latter into that which is confused by the exigency
of the sign or mode and that made indeterminate by exigency of the thing
signified. (Cf. *Summae logicales*, ed. Mullaly, pp. 9-13). Vives seems to have
invented the category of 'mixed' from his own imagination.

42 This alphabetical pharmacopoeia of the logicians and their aspirations
to mathematics was ridiculed also in the *Praise of Folly*. "And how they
despise the vulgar crowd whenever they bring out their triangles, quadri-
laterals, circles and similar mathematical diagrams, piled on top of each
other and intertwined like a maze, and then letters of the alphabet which
they marshal in line and deploy hither and thither in order to throw dust
in the eyes of the less well-informed! Some of them too will also foretell
the future by consulting the stars, promising further wonderful marvels,
and they are lucky enough to find people who believe this too." Erasmus,
Praise of Folly, trans. Radice (Harmondsworth, 1971), p. 152.

who had taken up the study of geometry thought that a line designated B was posited determinately, while line A was, like himself, confused. For to his way of thinking A and B are so all-powerful that all the confused and chaotic disorder of hell, or of ancient Chaos itself, could be defined and clarified by simply calling it B, while on the contrary the magic letter A could overturn and confuse the orderly workings of the universe. But when they hear these arguments, they say without a moment's hesitation, "That is the way I mentally conceive of it," [43] which is exactly what they do in everything else, cleaning mud with mud. First of all, what is it but their own stupidity and perversity that makes their understanding of things conflict with accepted usage and the rational basis of speech? Secondly, however they "conceive" of it, their behavior is insolent and inhumane if they insist on using words known only to themselves and incomprehensible to everyone else.

Surely it is self-evident that techniques which have to do with speech do not concern themselves with the delirious and foolish fictions of a certain few, but rather with things that are familiar to all the speakers of that language. If some ignoramus should construe the statement, "You are blonde," [44] to mean that 'man is a lion', this would immediately be considered false, not true, because its true meaning must correspond with what it actually signifies in reality. As Cicero said so well in the first book of the *Laws*, "True and false, consequent and contrary, are proclaimed as such of themselves, and not through something else." [45] If this were not true, what would prevent anyone from saying that "boar" means "bear", or "ship" means "hat," [46] and in general insisting that words have meanings which correspond to his own erroneous understanding. They say, "That's what it denotes to me." "Yes," I answer, "that is what it denotes to you because you are ignorant, but to another more educated person it appears otherwise, and has its true meaning." "It's a question of words," they say. Granted, and it is precisely in the matter of words, which they would like to corrupt for their lack of understanding, that we are defending

---

[43] The reference here is to the conceptualists, whose greatest figure was William of Ockham. In their arguments mental entities (*intentiones*) or concepts were more important than words. According to the precepts of this school the usage of words as language signs was established simply by

studio dedisset, putasse lineam, quae signabatur per b. positam determinate, quae uero per a. eodem modo se habere, quo ipse, uidelicet, confuse tantum. Nam a. & b. tantarum sunt uirium, ut totum confusum & indiscretum ordinem, aut infernorum aut illius
5 antiqui chaos unicum b. praepositum possit reddere discretum & determinatum, & e contrario, rectissimum coelorum ordinem solum a. possit inuertere atque confundere. Verum haec ipsi quum audiunt, ilico dicunt: 'Ego sic mente concipio,' hoc est plane, quod in reliquis quoque faciunt, lutum luto purgare. Primum, quis, nisi
10 eorum stultitia & peruersitas, iubet eos ad eum modum intelligere contra omnem usum rationemque loquendi? Deinde, quamuis ita concipiant, insolenter atque adeo parum humane agunt, si sermone sibi solis noto proferant, & non aliorum more.

Tum etiam, quis non uidet artes, quae de sermone sunt, non ea
15 tractare neque curare, quae unusquisque uel delirans, uel ineptiens sibi confinxit, sed ea quibus homines omnes utuntur, qui sermonem illum loquuntur? An si ignarus aliquis, per pronuntiatum hoc: 'Tu est flauus,' intellexerit hominem esse leonem, protinus illud falsum erit, & non potius uerum, quia ex suo uero significatu ita
20 significat quemadmodum est in ipsa re? Nam sicut praeclare in libro *De legibus* primo inquit Cicero: 'Vera & falsa & consequentia & contraria, sua sponte, non aliena, dicantur.' Id ni ita esset, quid superest, nisi ut sunt isti latinae linguae imperitissimi, si quis ursum intelligat per aprum, & per galerum nauem, uelint quoque uocabula
25 ad eum modum significare, quo ille praue intelligit? Mihi, inquit, ita notat; tibi uero, quia ignarus, at alii docto, & ex sua uera significatione secus. Quaestio est de uerbis, inquiunt. Et uere de uerbis, quae quia non capiunt, corrumpere uolunt, nos defendimus.

---

5 praepositum] praesuppositum S   12 insolenter] *add.* inciviliter S   17
pronuntiatum] profatum S   22 dicantur] indicantur S

---

convention (*secundum placitum instituentis*), whereas the mental term derived its meaning from nature. Cf. Ernest A. Moody, *Truth and Consequence in Medieval Logic* (Amsterdam, 1953), p. 19.

[44] The Latin adjective "flavus" was usually used of a lion, hence the semantic confusion in this instance.

[45] Cicero, *De legibus*, I. 17.45.

[46] Confusion between *galera*, related to the common Latin word *galea*, a headpiece, and *galera*, a word derived from medieval Greek meaning a ship.

ourselves. But if everyone were to invent his own language, declaring that words mean what he wants them to mean, what use would there be for learning any language at all, not to mention Latin? It would be much easier in the end to have words mean whatever we should like them to mean. There will be as many different meanings as there are people thinking or "conceiving" of them, so that finally no one will understand anyone else, since everyone will be using words in his own way rather than in the commonly accepted way.

Then, if anyone should object, it will merely be a question of words, which you grave philosophers pretend to despise in your logical disputations, as if logic were natural or moral philosophy, which subordinates words to meaning and content, rather than an art which has to do precisely with words. What is your whole sophistic discipline but a system of verbal quibbling dependent on the distorted meaning of words? But if you say that you do not concern yourselves with words, do you not see that your whole cloud of sophisms has been dissipated with a single word? But they do not make this assertion until someone catches them in the erroneous meanings of a word stemming from their ignorance. What if they were to impose the same rules, which they now claim for logic as they conceive it, on grammar and rhetoric as well, and were to transfer their meaningless tricks into these arts and order the grammarian to talk as they do, so that their own language would seem to conform more closely to good Latinity? I see no other way in which they could defend these statements by whatever kind of logic, true or false, since they claim at the very beginning of their course that truth and falsehood require suitable language, that is to say, language free of solecisms, not to mention barbarisms. To give an example: if they conceive that the man who is drunk on wine has not drunk the wine which is in India, why do they not say, with more simplicity and common sense: "This man does not drink of the wine which is in India," or "there is some wine which this man does not drink," or "This man does not drink all wine," or even, "There is some wine which he does not drink?" Similarly, why don't they say: "You are not some man," or "You are not all man," rather than "You are not man," which in the general interpretation would mean that the person referred to is not a man?

Quod si legem unusquisque de uerbis feret, ut apud se significant,
quid attinet, non dico latinam linguam, sed ne ullam prorsus
addiscere, quum illud facilius sit uerba id demum significare, quod
unicuilibet uisum fuerit, & quot erunt mente concipientes, tam
5 uarios habebunt significatus. Ita tandem, ut nemo alterum intelligat,
quum unusquisque uerbis suo more utatur, non communi.

Tunc quoque si quis conqueratur, de uerbis erit quaestio, quam
uos grauissimi philosophi, quum de dialectica disputetis, contemnere
uos dictis, proinde ac dialectica naturalis, uel moralis esset philo-
10 sophia, quae modo rem & sensa teneat, negligit uerba, & non
potius sit ars, quae non de rebus aliis quam de uerbis disputat,
quasi uero tota uestra Sophistica illa disciplina aliud quicquam
sit, quam captiones ex deprauis verborum significationibus. Quod
si de his uos curare negatis, non uidetis totam uestram Sophismatum
15 nebulam uno uerbo discussam esse? Verum hoc ipsi non iactant
quousque uerborum corruptiones quas ex sua ignorantia faciunt
aliquis deprehendit. Adde quod si haec quam ita concipiunt, uolunt
dialecticen docere, imponant etiam eandem legem grammaticae &
rhetoricae, ac sua stulte excogitata in has quoque artes transfun-
20 dant, iubeant grammaticum more suo loqui, ut ea quae dicunt,
latinitati congrua esse uideantur. Nam alioqui non uideo qui possint
ea defendere dialectica, uera uel falsa, cum hoc isti in principio
suae artis affirment, uerum & falsum congruum sermonem exigere,
id est, plane sine soloecismis, ut de barbarismis taceam. Quid?
25 si concipiunt eum, qui sit uino inebriatus, uinum quod est in India
non bibisse, cur non proferunt simplicius, & ad hominum sensum
accomodatius: 'hic homo uinum quod est in India non bibit,' aut
sic: 'uinum aliquod est, quod hic homo non bibit,' aut: 'hic homo
non omne uinum bibit,' siue, 'nonnullum uinum non bibit.' Similiter
30 cur non dicunt? 'Tu nonnullus homo non es,' aut, 'non es omnis
homo,' potius quam 'tu homo non es,' per quam nemo est, qui non
intelligat, eum non esse hominem, de quo id dicitur.

---

15 uerbo] *add.* atque exiguo flatu S   26 sensum] *add.* atque intelligen-
tiam S

Likewise, if they want to say that every man is an animal, but not this or that animal, but that singular men are singular animals, what use is there in ferreting out obscure modes of expression, like "animal is every man," rather than the straight-forward "Every man is an animal?" Do they want bread that is better than that made with flour? I know what their answer will be, that in the simple, genuine, true and direct manner of speaking there is no room for cavilling, which is the primary goal of their investigation. Am I right? To find a point for quibbling you are prepared to destroy the whole edifice of language, like the men in a besieged city who demolished a great part of the wall to find a single mouse. But consider for a moment if you act reasonably. I ask you, what chance is there for verbal quibbling if you use words which you have invented at your own whim? If you call someone a man, and that word means "ass" to you, do you think he will be affected by the insult? If raillery, jokes, jeers, witticisms, insults and injuries are expressed in words that are privately invented by the speaker and unknown to anyone else, that would be ridiculous enough, but if their meaning is obscure, they are utterly absurd and pointless, and are worth nothing at all. Daphitas, Euthydemus, Dionysodo-rus,[47] and others who engaged in subtle verbal debates in antiquity used words and phrases which everyone else used, playing on their hidden and abstruse meanings, and in this way they deceived and foiled their opponents. When Aristotle himself treats of sophistic deception in the two volumes of his *On Sophistical Refutations*,[48] and explains ways to avoid every trick of sophism, not only those already discovered, but anticipating those yet to be invented, he reduces his teaching to the precepts and techniques proper to an art in his usual manner, extraordinary and indefatigable genius that he was. Yet he never mentions any sophistic arguments that are so ridiculous and irrelevant that they must achieve their deception through the medium of new and unusual words made up for the occasion, or rely on altered meanings of old words. At this point my opponents often object, shaking their heads with great hauteur: "Nouns have the meaning one wishes to give them." Fine, so be it, but by whose will and judgement will the meaning of nouns be determined? Roman nouns cannot have meanings

---

[47] Daphitas, a Cynic philosopher of whom very little is known, cited by Cicero in his *De fato*, and for that authority adduced here by Vives. Euthy-

Tum si uolunt dicere esse hominem omnem animal, non tamen
hoc unum animal aut illud, sed singulos homines esse singula
animalia, quid attinet litterulas exquirere, 'animal est omnis homo,'
potius quam sic rectius efferre, 'omnis homo est animal?' Quid?
5 quaeruntne meliorem panem quam triticeum? Scio quid dicent,
non esse in illo simplici, genuino, uero ac recto loquendi modo
locum cauillo qui ab ipsis in primis quaeritur. Ita ne? Vos ergo
ut cauillum inueniatis, totam sermonis rationem parati estis diruere,
ut illi qui ut murem unum pressi obsidione inuenirent, magnam
10 muri partem demoliebantur. Sed attendite, quam id prudenter a
uobis fiat. Quaenam, quaeso, potest patere occasio cauillationi in
uerbis, quae tu tibi arbitratu confinxisti tuo? Si enim hominem
aliquem appellares, et ea uox asinum tibi significaret, putas illum
iniuria affectum iri? Cauilli, ioci, scommata, dicteria, contumeliae,
15 iniuriae, si uerbis fiant, non dico ab eo qui dicit confictis, nemini
notis, nam hoc stultissimum est, sed si obscuris iactentur uerbis,
frigida & insulsa sunt, nihil plane ualent. Daphyta, Euthydemus,
Dionysodorus, & reliqui olim qui cauillabantur, uocabulis, orationibus, quibus utebantur omnes, subdola quadam & latenti
20 ratione ludentes, fallebant uersabantque respondentem. Aristoteles
ipse, quum duobus elenchorum uoluminibus sophisticas praestigias
tractet, uiamque illarum uitandarum aperiat, non earum modo,
quae iam antea fuerant, sed etiam quae inueniri postea poterant, ut
fuit uir ille diuino ingenio, indefesso & singulari, redactis omnibus
25 more suo in praecepta, formamque artis, nullius tamen unquam
adeo ridiculi seu potius impudentis sophistici elenchi meminit, qui
nouis inusitatisque uocabulis excogitatis, aut ueterum uerborum
significatione mutata eludere ac fallere tentaret. Et hoc loco subinde
illud detortis nutibus magno cum fastidio obiectant: 'Nomina
30 significant ad placitum'. Sane ita est, sed uidendum est tamen ex
quorum placito & uoluntate nomina significent. Non enim arbitrio

---

13 illum] eum S   24 ingenio] ingenio, indefessa & singulari diligentia S

---

demus of Chios, Sophist and older contemporary of Socrates, is represented
as a ridiculous figure in Plato's dialogue of that name. Dionysodorus,
brother of Euthydemus, shared the same infamous reputation.
48 It was the discovery and revived interest in the *On Sophistical Refutations* that inspired the sophistic direction of medieval logic, but as Vives
rightly affirms, the disciples betrayed the master in their hypersubtleties.

according to the discretion of Parthians or Indians, nor on the other hand can Parthian and Indian nouns have meanings bestowed upon them by Romans. Rather, Roman nouns are determined by Romans, and Parthian by Parthians.

If I were to profess a Vives logic, and you a Fort logic, and another man a Lax logic, and yet another a Dullaert logic, words would then have the meanings that we should like to give them. But if we all profess to teach Latin logic, words will have meaning according to the customs and usages of the Latins, and not according to us. It is senseless and offensive to use Gothic or Sarmatian [49] nouns in Latin logic, or worse yet, words conjured up in our own minds that belong to no people at all. I should like very much to hear what our distinguished colleagues would have to say if they were to teach logic in Spanish or French, which is just as conceivable as teaching it in Latin or Greek. Surely they would not make up rules at will instead of abiding by the grammatical structures of those languages. Would they want two negatives to make an affirmative, as is true of Latin, when in Spanish, French, and Greek, as in almost any language, two negatives have more force than one? But if they would be willing to accept the laws of the spoken language in teaching logic in a given language, and not introduce their own rules, why do they wish to exercise tyranny over the language of the free people of Rome, constraining this marvelous instrument to accept the rules of speech devised by their infantile and barbarous mentalities? That brings to mind a certain expression of theirs which they like to toss about, viz., *de rigore*.[50] They say that this statement, 'You are not man,' is false in a common-sense acceptance, but true *ad rigorem*. The reason for their insisting on this distinction is that they are lacking in common sense, and they speak only *in rigore*, a rigor more frigid than ice.[51] Moreover, they want this rigor to be understood, to be the objective of logicians only. Yet the fact is that although this word 'rigor' is constantly on their lips, I swear on my life that none of them knows what it is or where it exists. But in order that they may understand what

---

[49] The Sarmatians, a nomadic tribe originally from a region east of the Don, were closely related to the Scythians, and spoke a similar Indo-European language, far removed from Latin, of course, as Vives implies.

[50] This phrase corresponds in meaning to distinctions made by Ockham and others between 'de virtute sermonis' and 'ad usum loquentis' or between

Parthorum aut Indorum significant nomina Romana, nec e contrario, pro Romanorum libito significant Parthica uel Indica, sed
pro arbitrio Romanorum Romana, pro arbitrio Parthorum Parthica.

Si ego dialecticam Viuicam, Tu Forticam, ille Laxeam, alius
5 Dullardiam profitemur, certe ut nobis collibitum fuerit, uocabula
significabunt. Sin uero latinam dialecticam pollicemur omnes, ex
instituto moreque latinorum significabunt uoces, non ex nostro,
indignumque & stultum est in dialectica latina nominibus uti
Geticis aut Sarmaticis, ac ne iis quidem, sed uerbis nullarum
10 gentium a nobis exomniatis. Nam ex istis ipse peruellem audire, si
dialecticam uel hispane uel gallice essent tradituri, quod tam fieri
potest, quam latine aut graece. Num regulas suo ipsorum arbitratu,
& non potius ex ipsius sermonis ratione formarent? An quemadmodum in latina lingua duae negationes unam affirmationem
15 reddunt, ita & esse uellent in hispana, in gallica, in graeca, apud
quas, uti & apud reliquas fere omnes, negatio geminata maiorem
habet negandi uim quam simplex? Quod si in dialectica aliis
linguis tradenda, leges accipere ab ipso usitato sermone, non
ferrent, cur in lingua liberrimi populi Romani hanc uolunt exercere
20 tyrannidem, ut cogant ipsam a se hominibus infantissimis &
barbarissimis loquendi leges accipere? Huc pertinet illud quod
passim iactant, 'de rigore,' ut quod haec enuntiatio, 'Tu homo non
es', ad bonum quidem sensum sit falsa, ad rigorem autem uera;
idcirco ab eis conceditur, quia carent bono sensu, & cum solo rigore
25 loquuntur quauis glacie frigidiore. Ac uolunt quidem rigorem hunc
a solis dialecticis & intelligi & peti, & quamlibet nihil magis
habeant in ore quam rigorem, moriar tamen, si ullus illorum scit
quid est hic rigor, & ubi situs est. Sed ut intelligant, quod ipsi

---

4 ego] ergo S   10 exomniatis] exominiatis V

---

speaking 'logice' and 'naturaliter'. Of course, it is this very unnaturalness
of logical discourse that is the butt of Vives' satire. The proposition 'Tu
homo non es', as it stands, is 'in rigore' true, if one makes rigorous application
of the rules governing supposition and the descent to singulars. In that the
term 'homo' appears *before* the word 'non', it is not governed by 'non'.
As a result since there is no quantifier governing 'homo' it is taken as being
in determinate supposition, and following the rules for valid descent dis-
junctively, the proposition will be true, *de rigore*, but false *ad bonum quidem
sensum*, as Vives says.
[51] The pun in Latin is on the two words *rigore* and *frigore*.

they are all ignorant of, and may use the term more accurately and more judiciously in the future, I shall teach them the true meaning of this word rigor, which they bandy about so loosely.

Every language has its own peculiar way of putting things, which is expressed by the Greek word *idioma*.[52] Words have a particular meaning and force that is often abused by the unlearned masses, and even by the learned who make certain concessions to the multitude in the use of language. With the learned this occurs with less frequency and mostly in philosophical and abstruse matters, of which the common people do not have an exact notion. I shall give an example from Cicero, taken from his treatise *On Fate*, to illustrate this: "We therefore abuse the ordinary manner of speaking when we say that someone wants or does not want something without reason," [53] when what we really mean is "without any exterior or previous reason," not "without any reason at all"; or when we speak of an empty vase, we do not talk as physicists, according to whom nature abhors a vacuum; what we really mean is that the vase is without water, wine or oil." Such are the words of the master, in which it is clear that, *in rigore*, i.e., in the strict and un-adulterated interpretation of the words, the statement, "This amphora is empty," is false, and likewise "You want something without reason." Yet in the common acceptance of the words, these statements can sometimes be true. Thus thir rigor is an exact and unchanging norm of speech, and was well-named by those who first gave it that name, which signifies something hard, unbent, and perfectly straight. To define it exactly, it is that peculiar quality, that express, inborn and genuine power, that true and direct meaning of Latin sentences. And from what authors are ignorant men to look for this quality? Not from Cicero, nor Quintilian, nor even Boethius, Latins worthy of our belief in matters pertaining to Latin, but from Peter of Spain or whoever preceded him. There seems to be some dispute about who first invented these suppositions, extensions, restrictions, appellations, and exponibles, which as though issuing from the Trojan horse, have brought about the ruin and desecration of all speech and all humane studies.

---

[52] The Greek word *idioma* refers properly to the unique feature of anything, and by transfer, to peculiarities of language.
[53] Cicero, *De fato*, 11.33.

omnes ignorant, prudentiusque posthac & aptius uti possint ipso rigore, docebo eos quid sibi uelit rigor hic, quem toties in ore habent.

Est in unaquaque lingua sua loquendi proprietas, quod a graecis
5 ἰδίωμα dicitur. Sunt & uocibus sua significata, suae uires, quibus nonnunquam indoctior ipsa multitudo abutitur, doctiores indulgent utcunque plebi in sermonis usu, ipsi inter sese & aliter sentiunt & loquuntur, quamuis haec non usque adeo multa, & fere in philosophicis abditisque sint rebus, quas ipse populus non ita
10 exacte callet ut a philosophis intelliguntur. Dabo unum ex Cicerone exemplum, quo ipsa tota res intelligatur, qui in libro *De fato* ad hunc loquitur modum: 'Communi igitur consuetudine sermonis abutimur, quum ita dicimus, uelle aliquid quempiam, aut nolle sine causa, ut dicamus sine externa & antecedente causa, non sine
15 aliqua, ut cum uas inane dicitur, non ita loquimur ut physici, quibus inane esse nihil placet, sed ita ut, uerbi causa, sine aqua, sine uino, sine oleo uas esse dicamus: Haec ille, quibus ex uerbis apparet in rigore, id est in uero ac germano sermonis sensu, hoc pronuntiatum falsum esse, 'haec amphora est uacua.' Similiter &
20 hoc, 'tu aliquid uis sine causa,' sed ad sensum uulgarem uera illa nonnunquam esse, est ergo hic rigor ipsa exacta & inflexa loquendi norma. Nam tamquam res dura, infracta, & semper recta, appellatus est rigor, quam bene illi uiderint, qui primi sic appellarunt. Est ergo, ut apertius eloquar, ipsa proprietas, ipsa expressa, natiua
52 ac germana uis, ipse rectus uerusque sensus orationum latinarum. At hunc abs quibus auctoribus petunt homines ignari? Non a Cicerone, non a Quintiliano, non etiam a Boetio, hominibus latinis, quibus credi latinis in rebus oportet, sed a Petro Hispano, seu si quis fuit alius ante ipsum. Nam de hoc parum uideo constare, qui
30 confinxit eis suppositiones, ampliationes, restrictiones, appellationes, exponibilia. Ex quibus rebus, tamquam ex equo Troiano, totius sermonis & omnium bonarum artium incendium atque ruina exorta sunt.

Poor Cicero! Poor Quintilian! Poor Boethius![54] Poor Martianus Capella![55] If Peter of Spain knew the genius of the Latin language better than all of them! What kind of rigor is it, I ask you, that makes the sentence "You are not man" true, while it would be false to say, "An animal is every man;" [56] this one true, "The Anti-Christ who was, will be;" and this false, "Anti-Christ will be who was;" [57] and this false, "A star-seer is every man," while this is true, "Every man sees stars;" [58] not to mention worse examples? What man with any knowledge of Latin ever transmitted that kind of rigor? Will it be construed as true because Peter of Spain, who knew no Latin, dreamed it up? Are we to suppose that someone could teach the dialect of a given language (which is the real meaning of *dialektike*) when he does not know the standard language itself? One feels ashamed to talk any longer about "incipits" and "desi-nits".[59] Who was responsible for this subtle kind of rigor, these intricate examples, these obtuse trivialities? In what language were they conceived? Was it Greek, Latin, Spanish or French? Who ever said that a boy could not begin to learn an hour after he was brought to school? Well, the logicians say this is impossible,

---

[54] Boethius, *magister officiorum* of Theodoric, subsequently imprisoned and put to death by the same ruler. His translation into Latin of the *Organon* and his commentaries on the *Categories* and the *De Interpretatione* were invaluable to the medieval philosophers, and his own works on logic were much used in the schools. Other short scientific treatises of his nourished the teaching of the quadrivium, and his *De Trinitate* dominated theological discussions of that doctrine for several centuries.

[55] Martianus Capella, author of a very influential treatise, *The Marriage of Mercury and Philology*, an allegorical account of the ascent to heaven of Philology, accompanied by her handmaids, the Seven Liberal Arts, to be married to Mercury the god of Eloquence. Its chief appeal was as a useful compendium of information on the liberal or encyclopedic arts.

[56] The subtleties of truth or falsehood in these two phrases depend once again on word order. In the natural or common sense acceptance, the first statement would of course be considered false and the second true. But in the rigorous application of the rules of logic, the first sentence is false for the reasons given above in note 50.

[57] The position of the relative clause is what determines the truth or falsity of this sophism. The second version, 'Antichristus erit, qui fuit' is equivalent to saying 'Antichristus erit (true, by reason of divine revelation) et Antichristus fuit' (false). In the first proposition one may construe that there will be a time when Ant-christ will begin to exist. Then at some later time, Anti-christ will have existed. Thus the proposition, 'Antichristus qui fuit erit' is true.

[58] In the form 'Omnis homo videt astrum' the proposition is equivalent for the medievals to 'Omnis homo est videns astrum', i.e., if you can pick any man X, I can find a star-seer Y who is identical with that X, which is (or

O miserum Ciceronem, miserum Quintilianum, miserum Boetium, miserum Capellam si uim sermonis latini melius nouit Petrus Hispanus, quam ipsi omnes! Quis, quaeso, est iste rigor, quo haec enuntiatio est uera, 'Tu homo non es,' haec falsa, 'Animal est
5 omnis homo,' haec uera, 'Antichristus qui fuit, erit,' falsa haec, 'Antichristus erit, qui fuit,' ista falsa, 'Astrum uidens est omnis homo,' quum sit uera, 'Omnis homo uidet astrum,' ut alia taceam his peiora? Quis unquam eiusmodi rigorem tradidit, qui latine scierit? An quia Petrus Hispanus, qui latine inscientissimus fuit,
10 somniauit, idcirco & uerus erit? Perinde ac posset aliquis διάλεκτον alicuius sermonis, unde dicta est διαλεκτική, docere, qui sermonem illum ignoret? Iam & de 'incipit ac desinit' pudet loqui. Quis hunc tradidit tam subtilem rigorem, tam subtilia instantia, tam obtusa nugamenta? qua in lingua haec excogitata
15 sunt? an in graeca? an in latina? an in hispana? an in gallica? Quis unquam negauit puerum una hora posteaquam ad scholas ductus est, incipere discere? at isti negant, qui multa praeter-

---

at least could be) true. In the other reversed form, the *astrum videns* precedes the quantifier, and is thus not governed by it, and having no quantifier of its own, is in determinate supposition. The rigorous sense would be that there is some star-seer who is identical with every man, and hence that all men are identical with one another, which is false. The general principle involved in these cases is that words which have the power of exerting some logical influence on other words in the sentence do so to the right, never to the left. For that reason these sentences have to be 'unpacked', or expounded, as they said, in a particular order, from left to right.

[59] Norman Kretzmann proposes that William of Sherwood and Peter of Spain were the first to investigate the logico-semantic character of these words, which later became the object of subtle discussion. "Later logicians frequently discussed 'begins' and 'ceases'. References may be found in Prantl, *Geschichte der Logik im Abendlande*, to such discussions by Duns Scotus, William Ockham, John Buridan, Albert of Saxony, William Heytesbury, Marsilius of Inghen, Peter of Ailly, Paul of Venice, Peter of Mantua, Peter Tartaret, and Faventinus Menghus. See also Curtis Wilson, *Heytesbury*, Ch. 2, "De incipit et desinit". Wilson suggests that the starting point of this discussion is to be sought in the *Physica* of Aristotle, in particular Books VI and VIII (p. 29), and he is almost certainly right." William of Sherwood's *Treatise on Syncategorematic Words*, trans. Norman Kretzmann (Minneapolis, 1968), pp. 106-7. Vives came back to these vexing little words in his later treatise on pedagogy, humorously pointing out that even in the description of simple actions, one cannot make use of these words anymore, after their mutilation in the interests of logic. He says that as he is taking his first mouthful, he cannot really be said to be commencing to eat, because a whole series of instants would have already passed by. *De causis corruptarum artium*, Majansius, VI, 144.

because many instants have passed by after that first instant in which he began to learn. Likewise they say this is a false statement, "This stream is now beginning to appear," two or three hours after the water first began to flow. They do not admit these statements either: "This tree ceases to bloom" just a little while before it stops producing flowers altogether, or "A stream stops flowing," about a half-hour before it dries up. In this way they have contracted the meanings of the words 'incipit' and 'desinit' into such narrow limits that they cannot be used anymore. According to them, one could never say of anything at all that it is beginning or ceasing to be or to act; and all this because of the simple adverb "immediately" [60] which they have brought out of the midst of barbarity and to which they have attributed such astonishing powers, that it is capable of any meaning they wish to assign it.

What have they done but transform this beautiful Latin language into something as devoid of reason and common sense as those who thus defile it? Is such freedom to be allowed these barbarians in a language which is not their own? Immediately and unceasingly (if such is the will of the gods) they object: "Let us speak *in rigore.*" Let them speak *in frigore* if they so desire, and in ice itself, enough ice to freeze the hot baths of Nero.[61] As if they knew what this rigor was, or as if they had the right to define rigor even if they did know, or the right to define the true and genuine force of a language of which they are completely ignorant! Go and round up all these logicians with all their ironclad and frozen rigor, who presume to prescribe norms of speech for speakers of Latin, and see if they can decipher for me one page of Cicero, Quintilian, Pliny, Livy, or any other Latin writer, or even one of their theologians, Jerome, Ambrose, Hilary, Augustine, Cyprian. But I beseech all of you who go under this name to answer me this: if Cicero were to say that the statement, 'Socrates homo non est,' means categorically 'Socrates is not a man,' while Peter of Spain, or some other of

---

[60] According to the *De exponibilibus* of Peter of Spain, *immediate* is a syncategorematic term on which the exponibles, *incipit* and *desinit*, depend for their interpretation in a given proposition. Cf. *The Summulae Logicales* ed. Mullaly, pp. 114-119. The subtle use of this adverb is amply discussed in the chapter of Heytesbury's *Regule*, entitled "De incipit et desinit" Cf. Curtis Wilson, *op. cit.* pp. 42-44. Vives facetiously chides St. Augustine in the commentary to the *City of God* for not knowing the meaning of the word

fluxerunt instantia post primum illud quo discere incepit. Tum &
hanc falsam esse aiunt: 'Fons iste nunc incipit apparere, duabus
tribusue horis posteaquam aqua primum manare coepit.' Neque
hanc concedunt, 'Haec arbor desinit florere, paulo antequam finem
5 omnino faciat flores emittendi & fons desinit fluere una semihorula
antequam exiccetur.' Atque ita in angustum illorum uerborum
incipit & desinit significationes contraxerunt, ut iam nullus eorum
possit usus esse, credamque ad istorum legem de nulla prorsum re
dici posse, quod aut incipiat aut desinat quicquam uel esse uel
10 agere. Haec omnia propter aduerbium illud, 'Immediate,' quod ex
media barbarie productum, non est minus admirabilium uirium,
quam illa in quibus conclusum ipsum esse uolunt.

Nonne hoc est ex pulcherrima lingua latina facere sermonem
tam alienum ab omni ratione & sensu humano, quam illi ipsi sunt,
15 qui haec faciunt? Tantumne barbaris istis licere in alieno sermone?
Et protinus atque identidem (si diis placet) illud obiectant, 'Loqua-
mur in rigore.' Loquantur potius in frigore & in ipsa etiam glacie,
quae una satis esset ad maximas illas thermas Neronianas frige-
faciendas. Quasi uel scirent ipsi quid sit rigor, uel ipsorum esset,
20 etiam si scirent, diffinire rigorem, & ueram germanamque uim
illius linguae cuius sunt prorsus inscii. Cedo isti uniuersi cum suo
toto ferreo & gelidissimo rigore, qui latinis hominibus praescribere
uolunt leges loquendi, intelligant mihi folium unum uel Ciceronis,
uel Quintiliani, uel Plinii, uel Livii, uel cuiusquam alterius Latini
25 scriptoris, ne suorum quidem Theologorum, Hieronymi, Ambrosii,
Hilarii, Augustini, Cypriani. Verum obsecro uos omnes, quotquot
estis huius notae homines, dicat Cicero per enuntiationem hanc,
'Socrates homo non est,' significari Socratem nullum penitus
hominem esse; dicat siue Petrus Hispanus, siue quis alius ex

---

27 enuntiationem hanc] effatum hoc S

---

immediate: "Non intelligis quid sit immediate? Nimirum non est vocabulum
tui temporis, nostrum est, ut scias non solis Romanis licuisse in linguam
latinam." ("You don't know what *immediate* means? No wonder, for it is not
a word of your times; it is one of our own, just to show you that the Romans
were not the only ones to take liberties with the Latin language"). *Commentarium in libros De Civitate Dei* XIII, 2.
61 The luxury of the baths of Nero was proverbial. 'Quid thermis melius
Neronianis?' Martial, 7, 34, 5.

these sophists possibly more ignorant than he should say that it means 'there is some man who Socrates is not,' whom should we believe? Is there anyone so shameless and brazenly impudent that he would dare to maintain that in questions involving the nature of the Latin tongue we should have more faith in Peter of Spain than in the prince of Roman eloquence? It is from him that we must seek this rigor and not from Peter of Spain or the other sophists; and if they contradict Cicero, I think everyone will recognize who it is that deserves our belief in interpreting the meaning of Latin words. Since they are always contradicting him, and continually inverting and distorting everything, they should be frigidly deserted and derided together with all their insanity, and our obedience should be rendered to Cicero and other Latin authors. For if this rigor is not sought from those most learned in the Latin language, but rather left to the random invention of any ignoramus whatsoever, there will be no rigor at all, and everyone will present us with a logic fashioned after his own whims and feelings.

For that is exactly what they are doing when they give their opposing interpretations of words, each according to his own ignorant understanding. One school claims this type of supposition, another denies it; some explain implicit statements in one way, calling them exponibles,[62] while others maintain the exact opposite. Certainly when such matters are determined according to the whim and folly of ignorant men, everyone will wish to make show of his own inventiveness, and lord it over someone else. How can there be any art in this? Whatever comes into their minds while they are drinking or taking a bath is immediately made into an incontrovertible assertion, and they proceed to smear pages with black ink, and proclaim it as law, fighting to the death for their views, as if for hearth and home. You would have to kill such a person before he would think of desisting from his perverted conceptions. What I said about drinking and taking a bath was no joke, for I can show you a book of syllogisms (whose author you know very well) in which the third form of the second order, which is commonly called "festino", [63] was composed while the author was having a few drinks

---

[62] Peter of Spain thus defines this term: "An exponible proposition is a proposition having an obscure sense and a need for exposition because of

sophistis eo quoque indoctior, significari esse aliquem hominem
qui Socrates non sit, utri potius fidem haberi par est? An est
aliquis tam effrictae frontis, tam perditae impudentiae, qui dicere
audeat credi magis debere Petro Hispano in ui sermonis latini,
5 quam principi totius eloquentiae Romanae? Ergo rigor hic ab hoc
petendus est, non a Petro Hispano, atque aliis sophistis. Quod si
hi Ciceroni contraueniunt, quibus sit potius assentiendum in sensu
uerborum latinorum, quis non uidet? Quod quum semper faciant,
nusquam enim non inuertunt ac deprauant omnia, illi profecto
10 frigide cum sua insania deserendi deridendique sunt. Ciceroni uero
& aliis latinis auctoribus parendum. Etenim si non a peritissimis
latinae linguae petitur hic rigor, sed passim confingere indoctissimo
cuilibet licet, nec ullus erit rigor, & quilibet suo arbitratu atque
adeo libidine logicam nobis afferret.

15 Quod & satis isti faciunt, quum sensa uerborum diuersi explicant, unusquisque pro suo ignaro captu. Nam hi hoc genus
suppositionum asserunt, alii negant. Hi sic explicant implicitas
enuntiationes, quas exponibiles uocant, alii non item, sed contrario
modo. Quippe cum res pro insciorum hominum libito & intemperiis
20 iactetur, unusquisque sua uult inuenta ostentare, alienisque prae-
ferre. In quo quae ars esse potest? quum unus quiuis, quod inter
potandum aut balneandum ipsi in mentem uenit, extemplo asseue-
rat, & chartis illinit atris, uultque pro lege haberi, atque pro eo
digladiatur, tamquam pro aris & focis; citius hominem interficias,
25 quam prauam opinionem ab eo auertas & quia dixi inter potandum
& balneandum, ne quis putet id a me per lusum per iocumque dici,
librum ostendere possum syllogismorum, cuius auctorem tu optime
nosti, quorum secundi ordinis tertia forma, quae 'Festino' uulgo

---

11 auctoribus] authoribus B   24 citius] citiusque S   24 hominem] *add.*
non inuictum S   25 auertas] euellas S

---

something syncategorematic located in it, implicitly or explicitly, or in
some word, as in 'only man is animal', 'Socrates begins to be white', 'a
line is infinite', and so on." (trans. Mullaly, *op. cit.*, p. 104.).

⁵³ In current terminology the syllogism referred to in the mnemonic word
"festino" is designated as the third mood of the second figure. It consists
of a universal negative major and a particular affirmative minor leading
to a particular negative conclusion, as in: "No man is a stone, some pearl
is a stone; therefore some pearl is not a man." It reduces to the fourth mood
of the first figure (Ferio) by the conversion of the major.

at the baths of St. Martin [64] in the company of Arnoldus, Rocca and me. We kept humming to disturb the author, but he, taking the name "festino" literally, wrote it all down in his uncouth style, persevering into the dead of night, and on the next day before dawn it was ejected like an aborted fetus. Why should they not do such things and even worse, and with even more haste, when their whole art is to use no art, and to proceed along their own paths with the utmost liberty?

In their estimation, one has reached the peak of perfection when there is the widest possible divergence between his teaching and that of any predecessor. Let me make up some meaningless rule of my own and pronounce the following propositions: "An animal is man; a body is this stone." In a common-sense interpretation these statements would be accounted as true, but in rigor they would be false, according to the rule that I now propound: "Every statement in which a lower term is predicated of a higher one is false." [65] This is what my friends in Montaigu College did, who devised this formula for themselves to avoid my importune arguments: "Every statement in which *alter alius* [66] appears is impossible because of the way in which the terms are understood." They have provided very well for themselves with this formulation, and they could do this with impunity, for who could refute something that an ignorant person idly fabricates at his own whim? I could mention other more stupid examples; they will certainly not be able to reproach me without jeopardizing their whole contrived system. Why should I, who know some Latin, be given less credence than our fellow countryman, Peter of Spain, who had not the slightest glimmer of the Latin language?

But perhaps they will say: "You have no authority for making rules, but Peter of Spain did." A ridiculous answer, to be sure, and worthy of deluded, raving maniacs if the power to teach formulas in a language, let us say, French or Spanish, could be invested in a man born and brought up in far-off Scythia! Tell me, who ever

---

[64] The baths, or *estuves*, were a favorite haunt of the students.

[65] The words inferior and superior refer to the extension of terms; e.g., 'man' and 'animal' are related as inferior to superior, the men becoming included among the animals, and not vice-versa. The principle that Vives invents is, of course, invalid as it stands without all sorts of qualifications about negations, quantifiers, etc.

nuncupatur, inter pocula, in thermis sancti Martini, me, Arnoldo,
& Rocca praesentibus ac de industria cantillantibus, ut auctori
perstreperemus, ut ex nomine rem sortiretur uere festino, foeda
scribiligine exarata, & intempestive, tamquam abortus foetus,
5 postridie ante lucem eiecta est. Quid ni haec & peiora faciant
celeriusque? quorum est tota ars, nulla uti arte. Sed sibi unumquen-
que pro libito uiam facere, qua ingrediatur.

Ac tum demum se rem assequutum praeclaram existimare, quum
ab omnibus per omnia longe discrepat, nihilque sic tradit, ut ab
10 aliquo alio est antea traditum. Et ego nimirum, aliqua excogitata
uanissima regula, dicam has orationes; 'Animal est homo, corpus
est iste lapis,' quamuis in bono sensu tamquam uerae recipiantur,
in rigore tamen falsas esse, daboque hanc regulam: 'Omnem enuntiationem esse falsam, in qua praedicetur inferius de suo superiore,'
15 ut illi in gymnasio Montis acuti, quo nostra importuna fugerent
argumenta, formulam sibi commenti sunt: 'Omne pronuntiatum,
in quo esset alter alius esse impossible de forma acceptionis terminorum.' Consuluerunt bene sibi, nam & impune id eis facere
licebat. Quis enim rem, quae pro libidine ab unoquouis quamlibet
20 inscio uulgo fingitur, refutasset? Alia etiam stultiora ego com-
miniscar, reprobare certe nulla ratione poterunt, quin eadem omnia
ipsorum excogitata comminuantur. Et uideamus cur mihi homini,
qui utcunque latine scio, minus habebitur fidei, quam conterraneo
nostro Petro Hispano, qui ne umbram quidem latini sermonis
25 uiderat?

At fortassis inquient: 'Tu non habes auctoritatem faciendi regulas,
ut habebat Petrus Hispanus.' Ridiculum profecto responsum, &
uere hominum ineptissime delirantium, perinde quasi homini in
extrema Scythia nato & educato, auctoritas esse posset tradenda-
30 rum in sermone uel Gallico, uel Hispano formularum, quem ille
nunquam audiuerit. Quis, quaeso, auctoritatem hanc dedit Petro

---

1 nuncupatur] nuncupantur S   4 scribiligine] stribligine V   11 has
orationes] haec proloquia S

---

66 The expression *alter alius*, which seems to have been used by some
logicians, according to Vives, is a solecism, for *alter* means the other, the
second of the two, while *alius* refers to any other, and thus the two adjectives
cannot be used in conjunction with one another.

gave Peter of Spain the authority to create new rules in a language he did not know at first hand? And even if we admit that he knew a few words of it, he would know no more about the force of individual words than the Scythian, whom I just mentioned, would know about the essence of the Spanish language, which he had never seen written or heard spoken by anyone. I should not, however, account this as a vice of the individual, but rather of the times. I merely wonder about the sense of moderation of Peter of Spain and many others like him, that they should have decreed that their childish conceptions be made into laws in a language totally unknown to them. I should have hoped that, hearkening to the ancient precept of knowing oneself, they should not have strayed from their own domain unless they wanted to have that popular saying hurled against them, as indeed it often is: "Cobbler, stick to your last."

But I should like to know one thing from our friend, Peter of Spain, to mention one of our compatriots, or from whoever invented this elegant form of logic (for there are still those who think that it originated in Britain or Ireland [67] and was then nurtured and developed in Paris); at any rate, I should like to know from whoever it was why it is that all these suppositions, and expositions and the like, which they teach in their illogical logic, were never taught by Boethius, or by Aristotle himself. Why should they have devised all these categories with such presumptuousness, and prescribed meanings for the statements that are contrary to the whole nature of the Latin language, of which they have never had the slightest taste, nor smell for that matter? If their laws are true, then countless Latin sentences in Cicero, Varro, Quintilian, Pliny, Boethius, and other Latin writers, and Greek sentences in Aristotle, Plato, Theophrastus,[68] Carneades,[69] Chrysippus,[70] and other Greek writers will be found to be erroneous, because the authors were ignorant, not of what they were discussing, but of these suppositions, extensions and expositions. This will be so not only for

---

[67] The humanists usually traced the contagion of the schools to the 'barbari Britanni', who diffused their lethal subtleties to Paris and thence to the rest of the continent. Cf. Coluccio Salutati, *De laboribus Herculis* ed. Ullman (Tours, 1951) pp. 3-4.

[68] Theophrastus, pupil and successor of Aristotle, whose philosophical teachings do not deviate significantly from their model. His importance

Hispano, ut nouas ferret leges in lingua, quam ne de facie quidem norat, cuius etiam si nonnulla uocabula pronuntiabat, uim tamen cuiusquam uerbi non magis sciuit, quam ille de quo modo loquebar Scytha uim sermonis Hispani, cuius nec uerbum uel scriptum legit,
5 uel prolatum a quoquam audiuit. Quod ego sane hominis non dico fuisse uitium, sed illorum temporum. Modestiam tamen ipsius, ut aliorum permultorum, requiro, qui sua placita, sua plusquam pueriliter somniata, uolebant ilico pro lege esse in lingua ipsis ignotissima. Ac uoluissem juxta uetus praeceptum, ut sese nouissent,
10 nec pelliculam excessissent suam, ne in eos protinus iactatum esset illud ex triuio, quod iam fit passim; 'Ne sutor ultra crepidam.'

Verum ego a Petro isto Hispano, quamlibet nostrati, seu ab eo qui nobis hanc tam elegantem dialecticam peperit, (nam sunt qui putent haec primum in Britannia aut Hybernia orta, deinde Parisiis
15 alita atque aucta) ab illo igitur quisquis tandem fuit, peruelim audire, cur cum ipse suppositiones & expositiones illarum enuntiationum, atque horum similia, quae traduntur in parum logicalibus, nunquam a Boetio acceperit, Aristoteles ipse non praecipiat, tam impudenter illa confinxerit, & praescripserit sensus enuntiationum
20 contra rationem omnem sermonis latini? quem nec primis, ut dicunt, labris gustarat, nec summis olfecerat naribus. Cuius profecto leges uerae si sunt, in Cicerone, Varrone, Quintiliano, Plinio, Boetio, & aliis latinis, latinae orationes innumerae, in Aristotele, Platone, Theophrasto, Carneade, Chrysippo, & ceteris Graecis, graecae, non
25 ex ipsius rei, sed ex istarum suppositionum, ampliationum, expositionum ignoratione falsae inuenientur. Nec solum in Aristotelis

---

16 enuntiationum] profatorum S   23 latinae orationes innumerae] latina pronunciata innumera S   24 graecae] graeca S   26 falsae] falsa S

---

in medieval logic derives from his completing of the theory of the syllogism by the study of hypothetical and disjunctive propositions. The works of Theophrastus were a convenient systematic collection of opinions about the major problems of science and philosophy.

[69] Carneades, a philosopher of the second century B.C., founder of the New Academy, who argued that one can never assert the truth or falsity of anything but can only accept the greater or lesser probability of what is presented to the mind. He lived for some time in Rome, and his teaching made a deep impression upon Cicero.

[70] Chrysippus succeeded Cleanthes as head of the Stoa in 232 B.C., and maintained the orthodoxy of Stoic doctrine against the attacks of the Academy.

Aristotle's moral or natural philosophy, but even for his logic. Peter of Spain himself did not speak according to the norms which he invented. In fact, no one will be found either among learned men in general or among these pseudo-logicians in particular, who can speak so carefully that he will not contravene these senseless rules and forms. How could it not be so when these rules were contrived by them in opposition to every natural habit and custom of speech? Yet Aristotle in all his logic, never defined even the slightest rule which did not correspond to meanings inherent in the Greek language, as it was used by learned men, children, gossiping women, and the unlearned masses.

The logician does not create new rules or expound the true essence of language, but rather teaches rules that have been observed in inveterate and familiar usage, as I discussed previously. The logic of Aristotle consists in its entirety of a few brief precepts: viz., the nature of words as taught in the books of the *Categories*; the force of propositions in the *On Interpretation*; formulas for syllogisms in the *Prior Analytics*; their demonstration in the *Posterior Analytics*; the uses of persuasion and invention in the *Topics*; and subtle argumentation in the *On Sophistical Refutations*. Equipped with this tool, the young boy proceeds to the other arts and sciences, since disciplines that are learned for the sake of other disciplines (and logic is of this number) should not occupy his studies for too long a time, but only as long as is necessary to prepare him for the other disciplines. Aristotle does not embroil and detain his pupil in frigid and senseless suppositions, extensions, restrictions [71] and other petty terms. This great genius, the inventor of all those forms and syllogisms, and indeed of all logic itself, did not consider such things necessary for a training in logic. He considered them to be extrinsic to the nature of the art of logic in that they contradicted man's common sense and habits of speech. If he wanted to use all these petty terms, as our logicians do, what use was there in saying that a universal statement can be converted into a particular one,

---

[71] There is a separate treatise on restrictions in the *Summulae*, de Rijk, pp. 199-208; Mullally, pp. 46-61. The term is defined as the contraction of a common term from a greater to a lesser supposition ("Restrictio est coartatio termini communis a maiori suppositione ad minorem"). Extension, the opposite term, is synonymous with ampliation or amplification, and is the subject of a specific treatise in the *Summulae*, de Rijk, pp. 194-198; Mullally,

uel morali, uel naturali philosophia, sed in ipsa quoque dialectica.
Quid quod nec Petrus quidem ipse Hispanus ad eas quas tulit
normas locutus est? Nec est aliquis, non dico doctorum hominum,
sed ne istorum quidem Pseudo-dialecticorum, qui ita circunspecte
5 possit loqui, ut in suas uanissimas leges formasque passim non
peccet. Nec mirum, quippe sunt contra omnem loquendi consuetudinem & rationem ab istis somniatae. Atqui Aristoteles ne mini-
mam quidem regulam diffiniuit in tota sua dialectica, quae non
congrueret cum ipso sermonis graeci sensu, quo docti homines, quo
10 pueri, mulierculae, plebs denique uniuersa utebatur.

Neque enim dialecticus nouam facit traditque uim linguae, sed
ex uetere & usitatissima regulas obseruatas docet, quemadmodum
antea disserui. Cuius porro philosophi logica breuibus praeceptis
tota constat? dictionum uidelicet natura, quae docetur in libris
15 *Categoriarum*, enuntiationum uiribus quae in *Perihermenias*, tum
formulis collectionum, quae in *Prioribus Analyticis*, adiectis &
quae demonstrant in *Posterioribus*, & quae probabili suadent
ratione, quaeque ad inuentionem faciunt, in *Topicis*, & quae
astute cauillantur in *Elenchis*. Quo instrumento adiutum mox ad
20 reliquas artes scientiasque transmittit. Nam ea quae aliarum rerum
gratia discuntur, de quorum numero est dialectica, non diu occupare
studia debent, sed eatenus illis opera danda est, quatenus in iis
egemus artibus, quarum causa reliqua comparantur. Neque intricat
& detinet Aristoteles suum discipulum frigidissimis & stultissimis
25 suppositionibus, ampliationibus, restrictionibus, litterulis. Quae si
ad logicum instrumentum attinere uidisset, quis credat uirum &
ingenio & studio tanto, inuentorem illarum formarum, syllogismorum, atque adeo totius dialecticae fuisse praetermissurum?
Verum ipse non censuit illa tradenda praeter omnem rationem artis
30 dialecticae, utpote quibus communis hominum & sensus, & sermo
non modo non utatur, sed etiam refragetur. Quod si litterulis uti
uoluisset eo modo quo isti, quid attinebat dicere uniuersalem
enuntiationem in particularem conuerti? ut, 'Omnis uoluptas est

---

3 dico] modo S

---

pp. 39-43. It is defined as the extension of a common term from a lesser
supposition to a greater ("Ampliatio est extensio termini communis a
minori suppositione ad maiorem"). For further discussion of these terms
see de Rijk, *Logica modernorum* I, pp. 567-571.

as in the example: 'All pleasure is good', and 'Some good is pleasure'? Why didn't Aristotle express it more expeditiously: 'Good A
is all pleasure'? [72] When you (Aristotle) state that a particular
negative is not convertible, e.g. one cannot infer from: 'Some animal
is not man' to "Some man is not animal," what do you mean?

You see, these learned individuals, whom you once taught, are
now teaching you in turn, repaying you the favor, as it were, showing you how to convert according to this pattern: 'Every man B
is not an animal,' or, without using letters, with a statement of
the same quantification: 'Some man is not animal.' [73] Many of
them do not attempt to camouflage the futility of all this, but they
contend that such things should be learned because they sharpen
the boy's wits. Yes, of course! Is this the famous method of arith-
metic that Pythagoras [74] employed to test and exercise the minds
of his young students? Well, if he says that boy's wits are sharpened
by these studies, why do you old men teach these subjects to other
old men in theology? Is it your aim to ridicule this grave and holy
discipline rather than teach it? [75] And true to your usual manner,
you make a mockery of serious matters and never fail to delude the
hopes of your listeners. I shall not mention those other misguided
individuals, who perpetuate the inane lessons of their youth in
the medical professions, at the great peril of the public well-being.
But I shall not pass over in silence the detriment to souls and to
religion in general that results from the learning and imparting of
these subjects in monasteries. Religious men, as they call themselves, who are often denied access to certain branches of secular
learning, are not ashamed to embrace these corruptions of the mind,
often with more fervor than laymen. There are some theologians
who think that there can be no exactitude of speech if it is not

---

[72] The inference 'All pleasure is good' to 'Some good is pleasure' is perfectly
valid according to the Aristotelian reading of universal affirmatives. It
is a *per accidens* conversion. What Vives ridicules is the medieval statement
of such a proposition with quantified predicates, as in 'Good A is all pleasure',
which is obviously false, since there is no good which is identical with every
pleasure.

[73] Once again in this medieval meddling with Aristotelian rules it is
the implicit quantifier in the predicate that makes for the equivocation.
'Some animal is not man' becomes 'Some animal is not (some) man'. Putting
those phrases back into Latin the illicit conversion is effected even more
easily thus: 'Non aliquod homo est aliquod animal', and since *non aliquod*
is equivalent to *omnis non*, we then get 'Omnis homo non est aliquod animal'.

bonum,' sic, 'aliquod bonum est uoluptas.' Cur non sic expeditius
uertebat Aristoteles? 'A bonum est omnis uoluptas.' Tum cum dicis
particularem negatiuam in se non recurrere, quod non bene colligat
quispiam, si dixerit, 'Aliquod animal non est homo, ergo, aliquis
5 homo non est animal,' quid facis?

En doctissimi isti quos 'tu prius docuisti, nunc quasi ἀντι-
πελαργοῦντες uicissim te docent sic conuertere, 'Omnis homo b.
animal non est,' aut etiam sine litteris in pronuntiatum eiusdem
quantitatis, 'Aliquis homo animal non est.' At multi ex istis non
10 dissimulant futilia esse haec omnia, uerum illa discenda uolunt,
quod puerorum acuant ingenia. Scilicet, est haec Arithmetica illa,
qua Pythagoras & probabat & exercebat, & excitabat suorum
ingenia adolescentium? Porro si puerorum ingenia dicet rebus
hisce acui, cur senes senibus in Theologia haec traditis? ut ludibrio
15 potius habere uideamini grauissimam & sanctissimam disciplinam
quam docere? Et facitis quidem more uestro, nusquam non etiam
in maxime seriis rebus ludentes, magnamque ubique deludentes
audientium spem, ut transeam quae quidam etiam praua consuetudine inducti, in medicam artem ex hac iuuenili stultitia inferunt,
20 maximo cum dispendio ualetudinis corporum humanorum. At illud
non tacebo, quanta cum iactura & animarum & totius religionis
haec a monachis discuntur docenturque, quos non pudet homines,
ut ipsi uocant, religiosos, & quibus disciplinis saecularibus nonnunquam interdicitur, has ingeniorum corruptelas amplecti, &
25 arctius frequenter ipsis profanis hominibus. Quin & sunt nonnulli
ex istis atque ex eorum numero qui theologi nominantur, qui nihil
putant acute posse dici, nisi sit hoc amarissimo condimento condi-

---

11 acuant] acuunt S

If one leaves the predicate-quantifier implicit, the result is 'Omnis homo
non est animal'.
    74 There were many legends concerning the teachings of Pythagoras, and
the importance of mathematics as a disciplinary tool.
    75 The transference of the cavilling and barbarous language of the logicians
to the realm of theology and the resulting obfuscation of the simple truths
of revelation was particularly offensive to the humanists. This resentment
of the specialized mode of discourse reserved for a classical elite is expressed
at the beginning of Erasmus' *Enchiridion*, published in 1515 (Allen, iii,
858, ll. 24 ff.) Cf. in this regard James Kelsey McConica, *English Humanists
and Reformation Politics under Henry VIII and Edward V* (Oxford, 1965),
pp. 16-18.

seasoned with this most bitter of condiments, adorned with horrid and rank barbarity, and stuffed with the vain devices of sophistry.

One of them had heard tell that Saint Augustine was a great logician, and when a certain book of the great Doctor of the Church came into his possession, he scanned it avidly to discover some case or some example. They say he was very surprised to find that in a man so skilled in logic there was not one word about asses or *alter alius*, nothing about examples, or cases, no reduplicatives, exclusives, or anything at all resembling the teaching of their logic textbooks. To think that a man of such subtle learning and keen argument in discussing the Trinity never speaks of complete and incomplete distribution, particularization, complete and incomplete singularization, mediate and immediate suppositions, which are part and parcel of those godlike syllogisms, without which the heretics would have long since destroyed our sacred faith in the Trinity. These syllogisms have also given us our store of paradoxes,[76] which may not match those of the Stoics in truth or piety, but certainly are more remarkable, as:

> "The Son of God is not God. The Holy Spirit is not the divine Essence. Every Son is the Father and every Son is not the Father. God is not the Father. The divine Essence generates the son, and the divine Essence generates nothing. The Holy Spirit is not the Holy Spirit. God the Father is one; He is his Son and He is not his Son." [77]

And although the Nicene Creed and the consensus of the whole church denies that there are many gods and many uncreated,

---

[76] The method of Zeno and his followers was to prove their own hypotheses by revealing absurdities in the contrary hypothesis. Four famous paradoxes concerned with motion and velocity are ascribed to Zeno. In the most famous example of Achilles and the tortoise, he argues that Achilles will never overtake a tortoise if he gives it any start at all, for he must first reach the point from which it started, but by that time the tortoise will have moved further. When he has covered that further distance that has been put between them the tortoise will again have moved on, and so on. Cf. W. K. C. Guthrie, *A History of Greek Philosophy* (Cambridge, 1965), pp. 86-91. In the *Praise of Folly*, Erasmus labels the Stoic paradoxes as commonplace and banal in comparison with the outlandish maxims of the theologians, of which he gives a few examples: "...that it is a lesser crime to butcher a thousand men than for a poor man to cobble his shoe on a single occasion on the Lord's day, and better to let the whole world perish down to the last crumb and stitch, as they say, than to tell a single tiny insignificant lie.' *Praise of Folly*, trans. Radice, p. 155-156.

tum, horrida atque inculta barbarie concinnatum, istis sophismatum
ineptissimis differtum tricis.

Fuit ipsorum quidam, qui cum fama & sermone hominum
accepisset Diuum Augustinum magnum fuisse dialecticum, in-
5 cidissetque in manus eius libellus quidam illius, auidus legit, ut
aliquem inde casum, aliquam instantiam arriperet. Miratum ferunt
ipsum in homine tam logico, ne uerbum quidem esse de asinis, &
alter alius, non de instantiis, non de casibus, non de reduplicatiuis
de exclusiuis, nec de aliqua ex iis rebus, quae traduntur in parum
10 seu paruis logicalibus. Quin quod homo subtilissimus acerque
disputator, quum de Trinitate dissereret, nullam fecerit mentionem
de distributione completa & incompleta, de particularizatione, de
singularizatione completa & incompleta, de suppositis mediatis &
immediatis, quibus syllogismi illi diuini fiunt, quis sine iam olim
15 haeretici totam nostram de Trinitate sanctissimam fidem fuissent
demoliti. Ex quibus etiam manant illa nostra non tam uera & pia,
quam illa erant Stoicorum, sed certe admirabiliora Paradoxa:
'Filius Dei Deus non est; Spiritus sanctus Essentia diuina non est;
Omnis filius est pater, & omnis filius non est pater; Deus non est
20 Pater; Essentia diuina generat Filium, & Essentia diuina nihil
generat; Spiritus sanctus Spiritus sanctus non est; Unus est Pater
Deus, ille est suus Filius, & non est suus Filius.' Et quamuis
symbolum Nycenum totiusque consensus ecclesiae neget, plures

---

2 differtum] defertum S   10 paruis] prauis S   15 totam nostram de
Trinitate sanctissimam fidem] illa nam que nobis rectius de Trinitate tradita
sunt S   23 Nycenum] Nicenum S

---

[77] The conflict between the tenets of philosophy and the truths of revelation had become particularly exacerbated in discussions of the Trinity.
Without wishing to renounce his faith in that doctrine, Ockham was also
unwilling to sacrifice the universal validity of logic. Thus, the rigidity of the
syllogism can yield heretical results: 'Omnis essentia divina est pater,
filius est essentia divina, ergo filius est pater.' (Ockham, *Summae Logicae*,
III, 1.5). Paternity and filiation refer to distinct realities and are therefore
predicated of the divine essence in a formally distinct way. Likewise,
paternity is not the essence: 'Pater non est Pater, eo quod Deus' i.e., that
by virtue of which he is Father is not that by virtue of which he is God.
The Father is really identical to the divine essence, but is formally distinguished from it by paternity. Vives asserts several times his adherence
to the more traditionalist approach to these theological problems, rooted
in St. Augustine's rule that faith should precede rational clarification.
For an excellent introduction to the nominalistic forms of theology, see
the article by Paul Vignaux in the *Dictionnaire de théologie catholique*,
Vol. 11, pp. 776-782.

almighty, eternal, and immense creators, these teachers insist strenuously in their invincible disputations that there are three Gods, and three uncreated, almighty, eternal, immense creators, contrary to the opinion of all the Fathers, despite its repugnance to Christian piety, against the will of all the angels and of God himself, and to the astonishment even of the devils, such is their blatant temerity. From the same seed and the same sowing they brought forth three Trinities, and the same number of divine substances, for as soon as one admits that there are three Gods, he must also admit, willy-nilly, that there are three Trinities and three divine Essences, no matter how he plays with the twisted meanings of words, and no matter how he juggles these words as in a throw of dice. But let me come back to my reader of Augustine.

He was equally surprised that in the treatment of baptism Augustine did not discuss those truly theological statements that are of such primary importance to our faith:

> Water is required for baptizing, and for baptizing water is required. Should the minimal amount of water that is required be given, or the minimal which is not required? the maximum which is required, or the maximum which is not required? the maximum which suffices (and) is not required, or the maximum which does not suffice and is not required? the minmum which suffices and is not required, or the minimum which neither suffices nor is required? [78]

and other such quasi-divine utterances, without which our piety cannot be razed (I mean, raised—I always make this mistake).[79] Everything else is destructive and these only constructive. According to them there would still be doubt concerning the number and the dimension of the drops of water the priest should use in baptizing an infant when water is lacking in the baptistry, if learned men had not written all this down. Though the priest be unaware of the fact, he baptizes in the faith of those learned men who handed down these teachings, and since they are written on the *Sentences*,[80] they are the support both of baptism and the whole fabric of our faith, which would otherwise crumble to its ruin. Such matters can be discussed and explained only by a doctor, it matters not

---

[78] Vives here ridicules the formulas devised by the scholastic theologians for the administration of baptism. Erasmus had taken them to task for their

increatos, omnipotentes, creatores, aeternos, immensos, isti tamen
inuictis suis concertationibus tres Deos, tres increatos, totidem
omnipotentes, creatores, aeternos, immensos esse strenue defen-
dunt, reclamantibus uniuersis patribus, repugnante pietate Chris-
5 tiana, inuitis Angelis omnibus cum ipso Deo, daemonibus etiam
confidentissimam istorum mirantibus temeritatem. Quin & par-
turiunt iam nobis eodem ex semine & satu tres Trinitates, totidem
diuinas usias. Profecto enim quisquis admiserit tres Deos esse, uelit,
nolit, tres etiam Trinitates, Essentias diuinas tres concedat necesse
10 est. Quomodocumque tandem uocabulorum deprauationibus luserit,
quodcumque in latus illa tamquam tesseras conuerterit. Sed ad
meum Augustinianum lectorem redeo.

Tum illud pariter mirabatur, quod cum de baptismo tractaret,
non disputarit de illis uere theologicis enuntiationibus, & in primis
15 necessariis fidei nostrae: 'Aqua requiritur ad baptizandum, & ad
baptizandum requiritur aqua. An detur minima aqua quae exigitur,
minima quae non exigitur, maxima quae requiritur, maxima quae
non requiritur, maxima quae sufficit non requiritur, maxima quae
nec sufficit nec requiritur, minima quae sufficit nec requiritur, mi-
20 nima quae nec sufficit nec requiritur,' et alia eiusmodi paene diuina,
sine quibus nostra pietas destrui non potest, construi dicere cogita-
bam, semper hic erro. Nam reliqua destruunt, haec, haec sola aedifi-
cant. Ita ut dubium adhuc esset, cum in sacro baptisterio deest
aqua, quot & quam magnis guttis aquae posset presbyter infantem
25 baptizare, nisi illa doctores scripsissent, quae quamuis sacerdos ignoret, nihilominus tamen baptisat, idque in fide doctorum, qui illa
tradiderunt, & ea ut sunt super sententias scripta, fulciunt cum
baptismum, tum etiam totam fidem, breui alioqui ruituram, quae
a nemine nec tractari nec proferri possunt, nisi sit doctor, quam

---

9 etiam] *om.* S   22 haec] *om.* S

---

attempt to apply to the sacraments the four Aristotelian types of cause. Cf.
Praise of Folly, p. 158.
   [79] The play on words in Latin is based on the two verbs, *destruo* and
construo.
   [80] Vives here refers to Ockham's *Commentarium super quattuor libros
Sententiarum*, facetiously pretending that the *Sentences* of Peter the Lombard
were the foundation of the faith, upon which (*super*) these teachings are
based.

how learned or unlearned, as long as he is a doctor. Getting back to our reader of Augustine, he ceased wondering about what he did not find, and concluded by a sound and shrewd conjecture that there was a good reason why Augustine had not conveyed these teachings. The reason was simply that he wrote in Latin, and these teachings cannot be expressed except in a barbarous and bulky language, bristling with grammatical improprieties and solecisms, the sole language that can be used for theological definition in the classroom. Many people have been so persuaded by this senseless and pernicious opinion that they think that philosophy and theology and the other arts cannot be taught in a pure, uncorrupted form of language.

If anything is written with a semblance of style, whatever its contents, these men in their stupidity and ignorance do not call it philosophy or theology, or law, or medicine, but label it grammar. As far as they are concerned, Cicero's *Offices* or *Paradoxes* or *Tusculan Disputations* or *Academics* are all grammar. The only thing that is not grammar is what they teach, because it is not subject to the laws of grammar and overflows with all the impurities of language. I hasten to agree with them on this point, for what they teach is certainly not grammar, not is it anything else. Scotus, Ockham, Paul of Venice, Heytesbury, Gregory of Rimini, Suiseth, Adam Woodham, and Buckingham,[81] were not grammarians, but philosophers and theologians, and therefore the logicians do not understand them. Cicero, Pliny, Jerome, and Ambrose are non-scholastic grammarians; let them be understood by grammarians. How is it possible, they say, for philosophy and theology and the other arts to be conveyed in such a terse and elegant style, and not in the non-Latin and impure, distorted language that they are used to? Have you ever heard anything more preposterous? If by God's favor I shall live for another ten years in reasonably

---

[81] John Duns Scotus (1265-1308), the Subtle Doctor, had written youthful commentaries on Aristotle's logical works, and a series of subtle disputations, entitled the *Quodlibetal Questions*. Gerard Manley Hopkins, a modern admirer of the Scottish philosopher, aptly characterizes him as "Of realty the rarest-veined unraveller." William of Ockham (c. 1280-1349), usually regarded as the founder of nominalism, author of a very influential *Summa of Logic*. Paul of Venice or Paolo Nicoletti da Udine (d. 1429), introduced English dialectics into Italy at the University of Padua at the beginning

doctus, ad rem non facit, doctorem esse oportet. Verum ille qui ea
se in Augustino haudquaquam inuenisse miratus est, protinus desiit
mirari, & causam cur illa Augustinus non tradidisset, bonis &
admodum certis coniecturis deprehendit, quod ille latine scripserit,
5 haec uero nisi pingui atque adeo barbaro modo tradi non possunt.
Nam hic sermo barbarismis & soloecismis scatens solus est, quo
res theologicae magistraliter diffiniri possunt. Atque in hanc
stultissimam & pestiferam opinionem plerique adducti sunt, ut
philosophiam, ut theologiam, ut reliquas artes incorrupto sermone
10 tradi non posse credant.

Si quid paulo cultius scriptum est, quodcunque sit eius argumentum, illud (tam inscii & stupidi sunt) non philosophiam, non
theologiam, non ius, non medicinam, sed grammaticam uocant.
Ciceronis uel *Officia*, uel *Paradoxa*, uel *Tusculanas quaestiones*, uel
15 *Academicas*, grammaticam esse dicunt. Solum id quod ipsi faciunt,
quia regulis grammaticis subditum non est, omnibus sermonis
sordibus mire redundans, grammatica non est, quod ego plane ita
esse fateor; etenim illud nec grammatica, nec aliud est. Scotus,
Ocham, Paulus Venetus, Hentisber, Gregorius Ariminensis, Suise-
20 thus, Adam Godam, Bockinham, non grammatici, sed philosophi
& theologi ab ipsis intelliguntur. Cicero, Plinius, Hieronymus,
Ambrosius, grammatici extra scholam sunt, a grammaticis intel-
ligantur. Qui enim, inquiunt, fieri potest ut terso illo atque eleganti
stilo, ne latine quidem, nec ulla propria germana, et non deprauata,
25 nec immunda lingua, Philosophia, Theologia, ceteraeque artes
perhibeantur? Quo quid potest insanius dici? quem errorem ego,
si decem annos ualetudine non prorsus aduersa Dei beneficio uixero,

---

19 Suisethus] *add.* Holchot, Simon de Londonaria S   27 decem] *add.*
posthac S

---

of the fifteenth century. William Heytesbury, member of an influential
group of logicians and mathematicians at Merton College, Oxford, in the mid-
fourteenth century. His contribution to the study of kinematics, the analysis
of movement in terms of distance and time, were particularly important.
Gregory of Rimini (d. 1358), general of the Hermits of St. Augustine, disciple
of Ockham. Richard Swineshead or Suiseth, one of the leading logicians
of the mid-fourteenth century, known especially for his *Liber calculationum*,
in which he discoursed on the sophismata of the science of calculations.
Adam Woodham or Godham (d. 1358), a Franciscan and follower of Ockham.
Thomas Buckingham (c. 1290-1351).

good health, I shall rid their minds of this error, not by arguments, but by example. But to return to my previous argument, am I to believe that a person's wit can be sharpened by something that is false, stupid, foolish, frivolous and unsound? Our minds are nurtured on firm and true things, and require solid substance. Insubstantial things make them swollen and give them only the appearance of good health, like swollen limbs in the body, which are a sign that both limbs and body are unhealthy. Similarly, I think the wits of the students are sharpened temporarily, only to lose their edge immediately on contact with other subject matter, no matter how slight, and to become duller than a pestle. Do these men think that there is so much time available for learning better things that we can afford to waste all this time in studies of this nature?

Poor foolish Theophrastus! to whom the Greeks gave the name divine, who once complained that human life was brief, and that there was not enough time available for learning the true disciplines which lead to wisdom and the good and happy life, and that when we were just beginning to know something, it was time to die. These men have so much time at their disposal that they can devote many good years to imbecillities worse than those of old women. Not only do they have free time for doing nothing, but it costs them much toil and travail to construct this system, which cannot be undone afterwards without an equal amount of work. But if inveterate illnesses cannot be cured suddenly or habits eradicated in a single effort, let us make some concession to routine, no matter how bad. Let those who are so eager to learn such subjects do so in a few months and discover what kind of madness it is. But let them take care in so doing, that they are not prevented from reaping the advantages of better studies by their indoctrination in distorted habits of speech, ugly barbarisms, and inverted meanings of words. I should not wish them to be of such tenacious memory that these perversions cannot easily be dispelled once they have taken root. I feel especially sorry for the lot of those who spend ten, sixteen, or twenty years and even their whole life in this pursuit. Wasted, sterile abilities, if you wish my opinion, destined to be used as straw, stalks, and husks rather than a fruitful crop. Occupied as they are with these fine subjects, they never have time to read Theophrastus, Plato or Pliny, or any good writers. What's

e mentibus illorum non argumentis sed ipsa re delebo. Ceterum ut
eodem redeam unde sum egressus, re falsa, re stulta, re inepta,
friuola, insana, credam ego acui ingenium cuiusquam? Solidis
uerisque rebus pascitur nostra mens, & firmum alimentum sumit,
5 inanibus uero etiam tumet, praefertque speciem quandam bonae
ualetudinis, ut tumentia in corpore membra, quum alioqui & haec
affectissima sint, & illa insanissima. Atque his ita credo exacui
discentium ingenia ut cum ad alia, quamlibet parua debiliaque
scindenda & penetranda accommodantur, tota ipsorum extemplo
10 rumpatur acies, fiatque pistillo retusior. Tum etiam, tantum putant
nobis isti homines superesse otii & temporis ad meliora discenda
ut iacturam nullam fieri existiment eius temporis quod huiusmodi
in rebus insumitur?

O stultum hominem Theophrastum, quem Graecia diuinum
15 appellavit, qui breuitatem uitae humanae querebaris, in qua tempus
non suppeteret ad ueras disciplinas, quae ad sapientiam, ad bene
beateque uiuendum perducerent, addiscendas, ita ut tum moriamur,
cum sapere aliquid incipimus. En tibi homines tam redundantes
tempore, ut etiam uacet eis multos bonos annos plusquam anilibus
20 deliriis impertiri, nec solum nihil agere & feriari, sed id multo
labore, molestissimo & assiduo negotio construere, quod post-
modum non minore destruendum sit. Verum si ueteres morbi
sanari repente non possunt, nec assueta res uno impetu conuelli,
detur sane aliquid consuetudini, pessimae licet, discantur haec ab
25 iis, qui ea tam scire auent, pauculis tamen mensibus, ut intelligant,
quanta sit insania. Ac uideant ii, qui id fecerint, ne praua loquendi
consuetudine, foeda barbarie ac inuersis uerborum sensis, in
meliorum disciplinarum fructu capiendo impediantur, nolimque
illos ita tenacis esse memoriae, ut eluere facile nequeant haec, semel
30 si adhaeserint. Illorum tamen ego in primis uices doleo, qui decem,
qui sedecim, qui uiginti annos, totam etiam interdum aetatem huic
impendunt rei. Misera atque sterilia ingenia, & mea sententia, ad
paleam, siliquas, aristas, non ad frugem nata. Atque his tam pulchris
rebus occupatis, nunquam uacat uel Theophrastum, uel Platonem,
35 uel Plinium, uel aliquem bonorum scriptorum legere. Quid haec

---

1 non] *add.* uerbis & S   20 impertiri] impartiri S   23 assueta res]
assuefatione altius impressa res S   25 ut intelligant] solum ut intelligant S

the use? Give me any two of the seven liberal arts, which they
profess to be a part of their curriculum, in virtue of their ambitious
title of professor. They do not even know who Aristotle is. They
have no first-hand knowledge either of his natural or moral philosophy, or even of his logic, which they shamelessly profess to teach
without having laid eyes on one of his books of logic.

There is not one of them who can define what part of logic deals
with invention and what part with judgement, and how the two
ought to be used. Even if they occupied themselves with the true
kind of logic, they should not linger over it for such a long period
of time. Logic is an art which is learned not for its own sake, but
in order to serve as a basis for the other arts, and be their hand-
maid, so to speak.[82] Therefore, no more effort is to be employed in
it than is necessary for the service that logic contributes to the
other arts. The man who wastes much of the day in the study of
logic, without going on to the other sciences, is no different than
the man who gets a sieve to sift flour and make bread, but spends
more time than is necessary in shaping and assembling the sieve.
A tool should be acquired quickly, and no more care should be
given to this preparation than is suitable for carrying out the task.
Whoever devotes long hours in preparing the tool, rather than
setting himself to the task for which the tool was prepared, acts
foolishly. The only precaution that must be taken is to see that
the tool is not defective, and will not hinder or delay the task.
Therefore, only that knowledge of the art of logic should be im-
parted which is necessary to insure that the other arts will not be
harmed by an insufficient knowledge of logic. Who can put up
with the man who confines himself forever within the limits of
logic? Who could tolerate a painter who spends all his time shaping
his brush and crushing colors, or a cobbler who does nothing but
sharpen his needles and his awls and his various knives, and twist,
wax and add horse bristles to his thread? Now if such habits cannot be tolerated in sound logic, which is in my estimation an art
not at all to be despised, how long will we endure that babbling
which is the corruptor of all the arts?

---

[82] In the *De tradendis disciplinis*, Vives complains that two years of the
philosophical training in Paris were devoted to logic, a discipline which
he considered a mere *instrumentum* or propaedeutic to other philosophical
subjects. Majansius, VI, p. 150.

dico? proferant mihi duas ex vii illis artibus liberalibus, quas ipsi
uniuersas ambitiosa sui magisterii appellatione profitentur, quas
ipsi didicerint. Nec ipsum certe Aristotelem, non dico in naturali
uel morali philosophia, sed ne in dialectica quidem, uel de facie
5 cognitum habent, quam sese tradere inuerecunde profitentur, quum
eam ipsi nunquam uiderint.

Neque est eorum aliquis, qui difinire sciat, quae pars dialectices
sit de inuentione, quae de iudicio, & quo modo duobus his uti
debeamus. Quid quod tametsi in ipsa bona ueraque dialectica
10 uersarentur, non tamen deberent tanto in ea tempore desidere. Ars
enim est dialectica, quae non sua causa addiscitur, sed ut reliquis
artibus adminiculum praestet, & quasi famuletur. Idcirco non est
in ea plus operae insumendum, quam satis est ad ceterarum artium
ministerium, quod dialectica exercet. Nam qui multam diem in
15 dialectica conterit, nec ad alias scientias se confert, non secus facit,
quam qui comparato cribro quo farinam excernat, panesque con-
ficiat, in eo aptando componendoque plus aequo immoratur.
Instrumentum comparari celeriter debet, & aliud in eo non curandum, quam ut sit operi faciendo accommodum. Inepte profecto
20 facit, quisquis in eo anxie componendo longum laborem adit, &
non protinus illi operi, propter quod instrumentum paratum est,
sese accingit, modo instrumentum illud operam morari atque
impedire suo aliquo uitio non possit. Nam alioqui curandum hoc in
primis esset. Itaque tanta est dialecticae artis accipienda cognitio,
25 quantum sat est ad efficiendum, ne illius ignoratio in reliquis
artibus nobis officere queat. Iam eum, qui perpetuo intra fines
illius se continet, ferre quid possit? Quis ferat pictorem in componendo penicillo, in terendis coloribus, sutorem in acubus, in
subulis, smiliis, ceterisque cultris acuendis, in torquendo inceran-
30 doque filo, in setis illi addendis, totam aetatem consumere? Quod
si haec etiam in bona dialectica ferenda non sunt, quae est equidem
ars neutiquam aspernanda, quantum erunt in illa omnium artium
corruptrice garrulitate ferenda?

---

13 quam satis] quam quantum satis S   29 smiliis] *om.* S

This is the way I feel about all this: just as that wise old man Cato once said that a penny is too much money for buying something which we do not need,[83] so even a half-hour is too much time spent in this vain and useless kind of logic. The proof that it is not an art is that every discipline and every art has been invented and designed for some purpose. For example, rhetoric, music, medicine, law, and various other disciplines are designed to be put into practice, so that learning may be translated into activity. Some other disciplines like astronomy, or that part of theology which is concerned with the contemplation of the divine majesty after the example of Magdalene in the gospel, are learned for mere knowledge. But what about that occult science of logic? Surely, it cannot be put to any practical use, for no one is so out of his mind and bereft of reason as to think that he could use those impressive sentences in his daily speech, for he would terrorize and chase away all his hearers, as if he had pronounced a bad omen. The only audience he has for his delirious ravings are the poor two-penny disciples who are used to these mysterious utterances, sitting in their louse-ridden corners, surrounded by stench and squalor. It should be clear even to the most dull person that if logic has been invented to be used by the other disciplines, then this logic which they teach, which cannot be put to use by the other disciplines, must be no logic at all. The teachers themselves with all their pride and vain ostentation would never claim that this logic could produce knowledge. Sufficient proof of this fact is that they have no knowledge, no good habits themselves, for their kind of logic does not leave the indelible mark left by the other arts and sciences to which we give the name of habit.[84] As soon as you leave school, all that smoke is dispersed by the slightest breeze, unless you have an exceptional memory. Those who have dedicated their whole lives to such pursuits retire into a frigid and stultified silence as they grow old and have abandoned forever all that scholastic shadowboxing and contentious altercation; then,

    Rare is their speech; and great their desire to be still [85]
Then will they veil their huge ignorant brows with the silence of wisdom. Poor fellows, what else could they do? All that scholastic-

---

    [83] Cato, *Libri ad filium*, 10.
    [84] In this sense the Latin word *habitus* translates a specific philosophical meaning of the Greek noun *hexis*, as it denotes a permanent condition or character resulting from practice.

Si meum iudicium requiris, ego profecto sic sentio, quemadmodum quod opus non est, emptum asse est carum, ut prudentissimus ille senex dicebat Cato, ita in hac inutili & uanissima dialectica uel unam consumptam semihoram esse nimis; quam quidem non esse
5 artem, uel illo argumento manifestum est, quod disciplina omnis, omnisque ars in aliquem usum est inuenta & comparata. Haec quidem, ut agamus, transeatque in operas eruditio, cuiusmodi sunt rhetorice, musice, medicina, iuris facultas, & reliquae permultae. Illa uero solum, ut sciamus, uelut astronomia, uelut illa pars theo-
10 logiae, quae contamplatione diuinae illius maiestatis, ut Magdalena illa contenta est. At ista tam recondita dialectice, quid, quaeso, docet? non profecto aliquid agere. Nam nemo est tam expers omnis sensus, tam a mente omni atque iudicio alienus, ut prodigiis illis enuntiationum uelit ullo in sermone uti, quibus, tamquam re
15 inauspicata & infausta, audientes omnes terreret & fugaret, nisi cum apud diobolarios suos discipulos eiusmodi monstris assuefactos, angulo quopiam pediculari foetoris & squalloris pleno, dementit deliratque. Quo clare quiuis uel stupidissimus perspiciat, quum dialectica eo inuenta sit, ut eius usus alias ad disciplinas accommo-
20 detur. Haec quam isti docent, ad reliquas disciplinas aduehi, aptarique non possit, fieri ut ea neutiquam dialectica sit. At scientiam ex hac dialectica expectari ne ipsius quidem praeceptores, quamlibet sint fastuosi, quamlibet ostentatores uani & iactabundi iubent; satis etiam indicat nullam in istis esse scientiam, quod nec
25 in eis habitus est ullus. Neque enim haec more ceterarum artium atque scientiarum sui firmum uestigium, quem habitum nominamus, post se relinquunt. Simul enim ac primum scholas exis, nisi tenacis-sima es memoria, totus ille fumus minima quaque aura discussus euanescit. Atque haec ipsa est causa, cur isti, qui tota aetate
30 eiusmodi rebus dediti fuerunt, quum senuere, scholasticasque illas umbratiles pugnas, & contentiosas altercationes sunt egressi, ubique frigidissime & stultissime tacent. Tunc, 'Rarus sermo illis, & magna libido tacendi.' Tunc, ingenti supercilio suae ignorantiae sapientiae silentium praetexunt. Quid facerent miseri? Scholastica

---

34 praetexunt] praetendunt, quod e sapientia profectum uidetur S

---

[85] Juvenal II, 14. This passage of the satire is directed at homosexuals who affect the role of philosophers with their laconic, mystifying speech and pretentious demeanor.

ism has vanished with the schools; they have nothing else to say. These men who could not be outdone by magpies or gossiping women in their talkativeness, and who were more vocal than Stentor, the Greek herald before Troy, now rival the fish in silence, and from the domesticated frogs that they once were, they now become harmless goldfinches.[86]

Those who were so loud and vociferous in the bustle of the schools, whose life breath would fail them sooner than their voices, when brought out from under their scholastic roofs into the gatherings of learned men, look so dumbfounded that you would think they had been brought up in the woods. They seem so mystified by the strangeness and unfamiliarity of everything that you would think they had been introduced into another world. So ignorant are they of life and common sense, so embarrassed, so tongue-tied, that if they were to do or say something, you would swear that they were not men at all. Their speech as well as their manners and actions are so removed from mankind that you would see no resemblance in them to other men except for their exterior form. The result is that in the conduct of business, fulfillment of duties, administration of public or private affairs, and in questions of personal feelings, they show as much ineptitude as a man of straw. The reason is that they have had no contact with the arts through which such abilities are learned. Among these we can count moral philosophy, which teaches us about the mind and human life, and lends grace to minds and manners; or history, which is the mother of learning and experience; or oratory, which both teaches and governs life and common sense; or the science of politics or economics, by which public and domestic affairs are regulated. If you speak to them in Latin, the language which they claim to possess in all its essence and rigor, or even in Spanish, or French, or whatever their native language happens to be, they will hardly understand you, and they will draw back from this newness of speech, because it is not addled with signs, letters, relatives, and asses. There is no Latin, no matter how unaffected, simple or crudely and colloquially written, which they can understand. For this reason

---

[86] A very similar description of the decrepitude of the logicians is found in More's letter to Dorp: "By a strange reversal of things, it happens that one who formerly placed every type of wisdom in argumentative verbosity has now in old age become a speechless infant, laughed at by everybody.

illa omnia simul cum scholis relicta sunt. Alia nulla habent quae
loquantur. Necesse est ut qui prius a nullis picis, a nullis mulierculis
garrulitate uincebantur, ipso etiam Stentore Graecorum apud
Troiam praecone uocaliores, tunc silentio pisces quoque uincant, &
5 ex nostratibus ranis fiant acanthiae.

Illi quidem, etiam in ipso scholarum feruore, ubi nihil potest
ipsis clamosius fieri, nihil loquacius, quos citius uita deficiat quam
uox, cum ad conuentum prudentiorum hominum ex scholastico
tecto educuntur, ita stupent ac si essent in siluis educati. Mira
10 ibi & insueta illis facies omnium rerum. In alium quendam orbem
perductos eos esse credas, ita usum uitae & communem sensum
ignorant. Ita impeditos, ita implicitos eos uideas, siue quid agant,
siue loquantur, ut illos non esse homines iures, adeo sicut sermo,
ita & mores & actus omnes ab homine abhorrent, ut nihil illis
15 cum ceteris hominibus commune praeter formam iudices. Hinc
quoque fit, ut negotiis gerendis, legationibus obeundis, admini-
strandis rebus aut publicis aut priuatis, tractandis populorum
animis ineptissimi sint, non plus in eiusmodi rebus ualeant, quam
homines foenei. Neque enim iis sese artibus tradunt, quibus haec
20 omnia percipiuntur, quaeque & animum & uitam humanam
instituunt, cuiusmodi est Philosophia moralis, quae mores men-
temque ornat; Historia, quae mater est rerum cognitionis & usus,
id est prudentiae; Oratoria, quae uitam sensumque communem &
docet & moderatur; Politica facultas, & Oeconomica, quibus
25 ciuitatum rerumque familiarum status & regimen constat. Eos
non dico latine si alloquaris, cum se unos uim & rigorem latini
sermonis tenere iactent, sed si hispane, si gallice, si uernacula &
patria quenque lingua, uix te intelligent, nouitatem sermonis
horrebunt, quia signis, litteris, relatiuis, asinis, non est refertus.
30 Nam latine nihil est tam inaffectate, tam inelaborate, tam con-
temptim, tam familiariter scriptum, quod isti capiant; quam etiam

---

5 ranis] cicadis S

He might attempt to cloak his stupidity with a haughty silence to take
the place of wisdom, but thereby he makes himself all the more ridiculous;
for one who but recently was more vociferous than Stentor now with just
the exact opposite vice becomes more reticent than a fish; and while others
are conversing, he sits there like a head without a tongue, like a mute mask
or a Hermes pillar." *op. cit.*, p. 40.

I suspect many of them will not comprehend this letter of mine, considering it something arcane and recondite, although I could not write anything in more clear and simple Latin. If many of them have unlearned their native tongue and the one which they imbibed with their nurse's milk, why should one be surprised that they have no grasp of Latin, which either they never learned, or if it was learned, has long since been corrupted by that sophistic corruption of everything that is good?

These and similar benefits are to be derived from this art, not to mention the loss of time, labor, language, morals and all common sense. I cannot be made to believe that these monstrous perversions, this gangrenous plague of the mind, this corruption of talent can last for very long. For almost five hundred years they have visited many evils on men's minds. It is time that the other arts together with the Latin language, which is their seed ground, should wake from their deep sleep. As Cicero said, "Time will destroy these false opinions, and will confirm the judgements of nature." [87] Men will not always be so badly off. Time itself will tear away these distortions, and will bring right and true things with it. It is not necessary for great champions to arise to put these absurdities to rest. Since they are fictitious, shadowy, and without solidarity or firmness, they will fall away of themselves, little by little, and dissolve. As soon as men of wisdom return to the schools, the memories of these sophisms will become silent and will perish. It is not possible that mortal men should wander in blindness forever; their minds will be opened gradually, and will issue from darkness into light, and in repudiation of such depraved and pernicious pastimes they will embrace true disciplines. I do not think that this day is far off, for these nebulous, illusory insanities have reached such proportions that they are struggling under their own weight, and have become unbearable to themselves and to others. Human intelligence once put up with this delirious nonsense, but not at such an advanced stage. They have now become heavier than our minds can endure in their quest for better things. They will crumble when they have reached the summit of insanity, and will burst when they cannot become further inflated, and with that sound their memory will perish with them.

---

[87] *De natura deorum*, 2, 2.5.

causam fore suspicor, cur hanc meam epistolam, tamquam rem
nimis sacram atque reconditam non multi ex ipsis attingent, cum
tamen nihil a me clarius, nihil apertius scribi latine potuerit.
Suum uero patrium sermonem, & quem a nutrice cum lacte suxe-
5 runt, cum sint ex istis plerique, qui dedicerint, cui mirum est eos
latinum non tenere, quem nunquam acceperunt, quem etiam si
optime accepissent, nihil tamen est quod non corruptisset illa
omnium bonarum rerum sophistica corruptela.

Sunt enim haec & similia huius artis commoda, ut tempus,
10 operam, linguam, mores, sensum humanum amittas, dum ista
sequeris. Haec tam praepostera portenta, has animorum gangraenas
& pestes, atque ingeniorum lues, adduci non possum, ut credam
diu duraturas. Iam satis superque quingentos fere per annos multa
mala mentibus hominum inuexerunt. Tempus est, ut simul cum
15 lingua latina, id est cum suo seminario, reliquae quoque artes tam
diu sopitae excitentur. 'Haec opinionum commenta,' ut inquit
Cicero, 'delebit dies, naturae iudicia confirmabit.' Non semper
cum hominibus male agetur. Tempus ipsum praua conuellet, recta
ueraque secum inferet. Itaque non egent haec tam inania multis
20 magnisque oppugnatoribus, ut pereant ipsa, ut sunt ficta, ut ad-
umbrata, ut nihil habent solidi, nihil firmi, ita paulatim per se
decident dissolventurque. Et memoria rerum istarum simul ac in
scholis homines paulo sapere melius coeperint, tota prorsus conti-
cescet ac interibit. Neque enim fieri potest, ut caeci semper mortales
25 errent. Aperientur sensim ingenia, & humanae mentes ex tenebris
in lucem profectae, reiectis tam prauis perniciosisque nugis, suas
amplexabuntur ueras disciplinas. Neque id procul abesse crediderim,
quum iam eo magnitudinis hae umbrae, caligines, insaniaeque
uenerint, ut mole laborent sua, sintque & aliis & sibi ipsae in-
30 tolerabiles. Ferebant olim utcunque humana ingenia gerras, &
deliramenta haec, sed non tam adulta, nunc grauiora sunt quam
ut ab animis nostris ad meliora sua sponte tendentibus ferri possit.
Ita ruitura breui, quum ad fastigium dementiae iam peruenerint,
& crepitura quam primum, cum magis intumescere nequeant,
35 simulque cum illo sonitu perituram memoriam eorum, quis non
uidet?

I have learned from my parents, from men of wisdom and through numerous experiences that bad habits cannot easily be changed for better ones through the efforts of one individual alone. It is necessary that they reach such a level of depravity that they become intolerable to everyone. At that point man's nature, repelled by the ugliness of the sight, tears it up by the roots, no matter how entrenched and ingrained the bad habit may be. So teaches the common proverb that the best order is born out of the most perverted state of things, and bad morals produce good laws. Our minds can put up with moderately bad morals and moderately bad circumstances, but they shrink from intolerable excesses of vice. An example is ready to hand in the Latin language, which survived as long as it was partially corrupted and had no defender, but was restored at long last to its true splendor only when it could not be obscured or corrupted any further. I am tempted to ask of these men that they quicken the pace of their mad excesses so as to become such a nuisance to everyone, scholarly and un-scholarly alike, that all will conspire to put an end to this madness of theirs. I think I see already the advent of this time; bright, outstanding, liberal talents arising among all the nations are spiritedly throwing off the yoke of this stupid and violent tyranny from their necks, and exhorting their fellow citizens to freedom. The world of letters will finally achieve that sweet liberty which has been absent for so many centuries, and in the future men will give fealty not to these frenzied, violent masters, but to those benignant and holy masters, the true arts and sciences.

It is my hope that either within twenty years this whole edifice, which they have reared with their empty and senseless babbling, will be consigned to the silence of everlasting night, or that whatever survives will be to the ignominy and disgrace of its authors. And as for me, my dear Fort, I feel immense gratitude to God for delivering me from Paris and, as it were, from Cimmerian darkness into the light, and for letting me see the true disciplines that are worthy of man, and for that reason often called the humanities. I am not so deranged or disloyal to myself that if I were not thor-oughly convinced after long and serious reflection that these disciplines were preferable, I would have exchanged the old for

Ego sane sic a parentibus, sic a prudentissimis uiris accepi, sic rerum usu ac experientiis didici compluribus, prauas consuetudines non facile in melius uiribus cuiusquam commutari, nisi cum ipsae in tantam prauitatem peruenerint, ut omnibus fiant intolerabiles.
5 Ita hominum natura tam foedam rem auersante, breui tota illa quamlibet radicata assuefactio reuellitur & antiquatur. Unde est illud uulgare hominum sermone prouerbium: 'Nasci optimum ordinem ex peruersissimo, bonasque leges ex malis moribus procreari.' Nam mediocriter malos mores, res mediocriter turpes
10 nostra ingenia utcunque ferunt. At uitii uehementium nimietatem refugiunt, pati nequeunt. Paratum est in latina lingua exemplum, quae quamdiu mediocriter fuit deprauata, perstitit, neque uindicem sui habuit ullum. At tum demum restituta suo splendori est, cum offuscari corrumpique magis non poterat. Ita & hos homines nescio
15 an fuerit satius precari, ut suas insanias alias super alias accumulantes, ita celeriter adaugeant, ut primo quoque tempore, non modo praeclaris ingeniis, sed etiam infimis sint uilitate sua fastidio, & ab omnibus conspiretur in perniciem istius amentiae. Quos iam ego quasi ex alto fieri strenue uideo. Erigunt enim sese apud nationes
20 omnes clara, excellentia, liberaque ingenia, impatientia seruitutis, & iugum hoc stultissimae ac uiolentissimae tyrannidis ex ceruicibus suis animose depellunt, ciuesque suos ad libertatem uocant, uindicabuntque totam prorsus litterariam ciuitatem in libertatem longe suauissimam, qua tot saeculis caruerunt, parebuntque non his
25 furentibus & uiolentis dominis, sed benignissimis & sanctissimis illis magistris, ueris artibus atque scientiis.

Ita futurum ante annos uiginti spero ut opera ista, quae tam inani stolidaque loquacitate isti ad ostentationem gloriamque congesserunt, aut in obscuro aeternam noctem silentiumque agant, aut si
30 qua forte extiterint, ad ignominiam potius, magnumque suorum auctorum dedecus uideantur. Atque ego quidem, mi Fortis, gratias & habeo & ago permagnas Deo, quod aliquando e Parisiis quasi ex Cimmeriis tenebris in lucem egressus sum, uidique quae essent illae disciplinae, quae homine dignae ac subinde humanae dicuntur.
35 Neque enim tam sum demens, tam de me ipso male meritus, ut si haec meliora magno & exacto iudicio non censuissem, clareque

---

11 paratum] promptum atque partum S   31 uideantur] inspiciantur S
34 ac subinde] ac sub subinde S

the new, the proven for the unproven, or the certain for the un-
certain. No one likes to admit that what he had struggled so long
to achieve proved in the end to be frivolous and trivial, and that
the uninterrupted effort of so many days and so many sleepless
nights was all a game. In the beginning this thought was so dis-
agreeable to me that I often turned my thoughts from better
things back to the old ways, to try to convince myself that I had
not wasted so many years in Paris. I have no doubt that this
message will be very unpleasant to many people, but I want them
to consider the lessons of experience. If one cannot be among that
number of perfect men who know everything themselves, let him
at least be accounted as one of those good men who listen to sound
advice, rather than one who neither knows anything himself, nor
listens to anyone's advice. If they do not wish to believe me, let
them trust older men and their own teachers, who will be quick
to condemn this madness if they are asked their opinion, and will
deplore the time which they wasted in these vain trivialities.

I have often heard Dullaert and Gaspar Lax, my teachers, whom
I should like to mention out of respect, complaining bitterly that
they had spent so many years in such futile and inane studies. If
this is so, how insane it is, damn it, not to listen to the advice of
old men? I have no doubt that unlearned young men, more garrulous than frogs and more pugnacious than fighting cocks, will
criticize me, but my one consolation is that old men will think well
of what I am saying, and will give me their commendation. As for
those rash and ignorant young men, they will approve and willingly
accept what they now despise when they reach the age of wisdom
(if God so ordains), and perhaps out of sentiments of compassion,
will pass on to their younger disciples the advice I give them now.
My dearest Fort, I pray you for the sake of our friendship and
your outstanding talents that you turn to better things, and as
your years admonish, renounce what you see to be a corrupting
influence. If it were not for your excellent memory, all this learning
would disappear, but since your memory is so good, it will be a hin-
drance in better pursuits, and will cause as much trouble in being
unlearned as it was in being learned. Convince yourself that it is
not worthy of another moment of your time, and cast it from you
decisively and energetically, so that it will not prove detrimental
to your talents. You will soon perceive that this brief life is better

conspexissem, fuissem uetera pro nouis, adepta pro nondum adeptis,
certa pro incertis commutaturus. Neque enim aliquis est, qui libens
resciat, quae magno labore nactus est, friuola & nugas esse meras,
& tam diuturnam molestamque operam tot dierum, tot insom-
5 nium noctium lusisse. Ita & mihi in principio id tam odiosum erat,
ut saepe a melioribus rebus cogitationem ad uetera mea auerterem,
ne mihi persuaderi posset mi Parisiis tot annis nihil egisse. Nec
dubito etiam, quin nuncius hic futurus sit plurimis odiosissimus,
uerum eos illud considerare oportet, credendum esse expertis. Et
10 qui esse nequeunt ex illo optimorum maximeque perfectorum
hominum genere, per sese qui omnia norunt, sint saltem ex illo
bonorum, parent qui recta monenti, ne ex ordine pessimorum fiant,
qui nec ipsi norunt, nec melius monentibus auscultant. Quod si
mihi credere nolunt, at senibus ipsi suisque praeceptoribus fidem
15 habeant, quos si rogent, audient damnantes furorem illum mentis,
deplorantes id tempus, quod in his gerris uanissimis inutiliter
contriuerunt.

Dullardum ego & Gasparem Laxem, praeceptores olim meos,
quos honoris gratia nomino, querentes saepe summo cum dolore
20 audiui, se tam multos annos rei tam futili atque inani impendisse.
Id si ita est, quae, malum, insania est, nolle parere senibus bene
monentibus? Atque illud me in hac epistola (quam non dubito
iuuenes imperitos, & quibusuis Citeriis loquaciores, pugnaciores
quibusuis gallinaceis, uituperaturos) consolatur, quod senes bene
25 de his, quae nunc dico, sentient, atque ea laudabunt. Et quae ipsi
modo iuuenes temerarii insipientes contemnunt, ea cum per aetatem
sapient (si Deus id eis dederit) & probabunt, & amplexabuntur,
& quae ego nunc eis consulo, ipsi forte miserti sequentium minori-
bus consulent seniores. Te uero, mi carissime Fortis, per amicitiam
30 nostram, per tuum praestantissimum animum ingeniumque precor,
ut quoniam tua aetas iam te admonet meliorum, uidesque aliud
illa non esse, quam hominum corruptelas, quae si non optima
memoria fueris, confestim excident, sin uero optima, impedimento
erunt in rebus melioribus, eruntque dediscenda non minori negotio,
35 quam fuerint parta. Vides digna non esse, in quibus uel temporis
insumatur punctum, quin potius ut ambabus manibus, omnibus
machinis procul reiiciantur, ne ingenio officiant. Vides aetatem

14 credere] fidem adhibere S   30 animum ingeniumque] animum atque
ingenium S

suited for the teaching of the true arts, and that before long those
who hold these posts will be scorned and mocked by everyone.
I exhort you, therefore, and I beg you to turn your steps from these
aberrations, sound the retreat, and turn to those things which are
worthy of man and worthy of your talent. Knowing your wisdom
and your inclination toward nobler pursuits, I have no doubt that
you will do as I ask. I shall consider it reward enough for this
verbose epistle if I shall have induced you to follow after the true
calling of your noble and extraordinary intelligence.

I have also written to you because I know that I shall not be
speaking to deaf ears, and also because if I have any good effect
on you, I can also hope to exercise an influence on a great number
of the young men who are your disciples. You have almost a paternal
duty to give them the best teaching possible, and you would be
failing in your duty and indeed, to speak quite frankly, you would
be committing a great injustice if you were to imbue them with
vain and meaningless skills. I usually lay the blame for all this on
teachers because young boys in complete ignorance, driven to
them by chance as if caught in a storm, are overwhelmed, corrupted, and drowned in this sea before they have an opportunity
to judge for themselves what is true or what is false. At the same
time, I do not like to blame the teachers so much, who for the most
part are children themselves and scarcely know their right hand
from their left. These days they are brought into the schools right
after they have been hatched. They become teachers or tutors while
it is they themselves who need a teacher and tutor, pedagogue and
rod. And yet these same individuals (God forgive them) have re-
ceived the title of philosopher before they even know their own
names.[88]

I do not blame them so much as the directors of schools, whose
long experience should have taught them what is detrimental to
youth. Perhaps they think they cannot make a living in any other

---

[88] Vives ridicules the accumulation of titles, prerogatives and insignia
which the logicians arrogated to themselves in the *Exercitatio linguae latinae*,
Majansius, I, 283-408. These posturings were a favorite target of the
humanists. "...they think themselves nearest to the gods whenever they
are reverently addressed as "our masters", a title which holds as much
meaning for them as the 'tetragram' does for the Jews. Consequently,

breuem multo satius esse ueris artibus tradere. Vides breui illa
qui habuerint, fore omnibus despectui atque ludibrior. Hortor
itaque te & rogo, tempestiue pedem ab illis dementiis ut referas,
canas receptui, conferas te ad ea, quae sunt homine, quae sunt
5 ingenio tuo digna.

Quod, quoniam prudentiam animumque tuum ad optima quaeque
propensum noui, non dubito te facturum. Satisque magnum fecero
hac tam uerbosa epistola fructum, si te talem amicum adduxero,
quo uides a nobili atque egregia istius mentis tuae natura uocari.
10 Scripsi quoque ad te eam ob causam, quoniam scio me non canta-
turum surdis, tum etiam quod cum in te profecero, proficiam pariter
in ista multitudine iuuenum, quae te sectatur, quos omnes cum
patria quadam caritate complexurus sis, & optima quaeque
instituturus, parum satisfacies muneri tuo, quin, ut aperte loquar,
15 magnum scelus flagitiumque committes, si illos uanissimis stultis-
simisque imbuerit artibus. Etenim ego huiusce rei culpam in
praeceptores reiicere soleo, qui haec tradunt. Nam ignari rerum
omnium pueri, ad eos tamquam ad tempestatem quandam casu
delati, prius circumueniuntur, prius inficiuntur, prius hoc in mari
20 submerguntur, quam liceat eis quid rectum, quid prauum sit
diiudicare. Quamuis non tam culpem ipsos praeceptores, qui magna
ex parte pueri sunt, & uix sciunt utra manus sit sua dextra, nunc
primum ex ouo in scholas producti, qui potius ipsi praeceptore &
institutore ac paedagogo ferulaque egent, quam ut boni esse queant
25 institutores & magistri, atque isti (si diis placet) suum nomen quum
ignorent, philosophi appellationem iam receperunt. Non ergo tam
hos reprehenderim, quam ipsos gymnasiarchas, quos aetate, quos
longo rerum usu edoctos oportuit, qualia sint ista, quae suis in
scholis maximo cum detrimento & damno totius iuuentutis tradi
30 non sinunt modo, sed iubent quoque.

Credo quod non arbitrantur alioqui se quaestum facturos, quod
tamen quam possint sine magno crimine facere, uiderint ipsi, ho-

---

they say it's unlawful to write MAGISTER NOSTER except in capital
letters, and if anyone inverts the order and says *noster magister* he destroys
the entire majesty of the theologians' title at a single blow." Erasmus, *Praise
of Folly*, p. 163. Ulrich von Hutten also derides the doctors of theology
for the assumption of the title *magister noster*, as if they were the vicars
of the true master, Jesus Christ, himself. *Epistolae Obscurorum Virorum*,
ed. F. G. Stokes (London, 1925), p. 6.

way, but as theologians they should find out for themselves how it can be done in a less reproachful way. It seems to me that God will require a severe account of them for the loss of so much good time, and for the bad effects they have had on youthful minds entrusted to their hands. Who does not believe that grave penalties await the man who imposes himself on an innocent and unknowing boy for the sake of money? And what of those who destroy the lives and minds of boys? Will they go unpunished? That you may be aware that this situation has gone beyond the limit of toleration and has become a heavy and intolerable burden in the sight of God and man, I must confide to you that, the more religious and the more holy these directors of schools wish to appear, the more they order their schools to resound with the clamor of this fury and madness; and they do this with more seriousness than Zeno [89] ever expected in his rigid concept of virtue. I want you, my dear Fort, as well as all others who so wish, to evaluate the present state of affairs. Does it not seem to you that the school of Paris, like an old woman after her eightieth year, is showing the signs of old age? Do you think there is any doubt that within a short time it will disappear, unless by some art, that is, through the kindness of the good disciplines, it should be rejuvenated? (May God prevent such a fate; I shudder at the very thought). I should be willing to swear solemnly that there is no one so dull-witted and impenetrably ignorant that he would bring his children to that school to be educated, if he knew what was being taught there.

Come now, how many men of learning send their children there or confide them to these sophists? No one is so blind, so deranged, so neglectful or ill-disposed toward his children as to do such a thing; if anyone does send his children to Paris, it is not to the sophists that he sends them, but to certain other teachers who manage to retain some degree of wisdom in the midst of so many lunatics. If someone should suppose that I sound a little irritated, he is right, for I cannot talk about this matter without great feelings of regret at the thought of so many good hours wasted. I do not want to cast the blame entirely upon the teachers in order not to seem ungrateful in the eyes of some thoughtless individual, as I give vent to my indignation. If this letter falls into the hands of these men, and they can persuade themselves to read it, and if they are capable of understanding it, as is my fond wish, I have

mines theologi. Nihi profecto ab his maxime tantae iacturae tam
boni temporis & animorum iuuentutis, quae illorum curae tradita
est, Deus postulaturus acerbeque rationem exacturus uidetur. Quis
enim non credat manere graues cruciatus eum, qui innocenti &
5 inscio puero propter solam pecuniam imposuerit ? & hos qui
puerorum tempus, qui uitam, qui animum perdunt, immunes fore ?
Et quo uideas hanc rem ad summam suae impudentiae uenisse, ut
iam grauis atque intolerabilis & Deo & hominibus sit, quo reli-
giosiores, quo sanctiores uolunt gymnasiarchae uideri, eo magis
10 scholas suas his furoris insaniaeque clamoribus perstrepere iubent.
Illaque maiore exercent supercilio, quam unquam Zeno fecit
rigidissima sua uirtute tradenda. Te ipsum, mi Fortis, atque alium
quemuis, neque enim recuso, quenquam iudicem facio, num non
tibi Parisiensis schola tamquam anus quaedam post octingentesi-
15 mum suae aetatis annum cum tanto senio summe delirare uidetur ?
Num non eam censes nisi arte aliqua, id est beneficio bonarum
disciplinarum repubescat, quod Deus ipse omen auertat, horret
animus dicere, breui interituram ? Ego enim id ausim persancte
deierare, fore neminem tam hebetem & crassum hominem, qui
20 liberos suos ad eam eruditionis gratia deduceret, si intelligeret,
quae in ipsa docentur.

Cedo, quotusquisque ex doctis hominibus suos filios uel istuc,
uel ad hos sophistas mittit ? Nemo tam caecus est, nemo tam insanit,
nemo tam filios uel negligit uel odit. Si quis ex iis istuc mittit, non
25 ad sophistas mittit sed ad nonnullos, qui melius inter tot desipientes
sapiunt. Si quis me cum stomacho loqui putat, is recte sentit. Neque
enim de ea re summo sine dolore loqui possum, quae tam multas
bonas horas me tam male collocare coegit. Nolo in praeceptores culpam reiicere, ne dum iusto meo indulgeo dolori, alicui parum fortas-
30 sis prudenti minus esse gratus uidear; nec dubito quin haec epistola
si in manus istorum hominum uenerit, ac poterint sibi imperare ut
perlegant, fueritque ab eis intellecta, quod maxime cupio, sit

---

10 iubent] imperant S   15 summe delirare uidetur] summe uideatur delirare S   19 deierare] deierate V

---

[89] Zeno, the founder of the Stoic school, to be distinguished from Zeno
of Elea mentioned in a previous note, made virtue the keystone of his whole
philosophy. His teaching may be summed up in Seneca's motto: "nec
philosophia sine virtute est, nec sine philosophia virtus."

no doubt that it will offend many. Yet I think I may rightly ask of those who will be offended that they believe me when I say that I have not spoken of anyone in particular; I beg them also not to be offended by my words, but rather weigh the matter and consider my intention. But if all that I have said does not convince some of them, then all well and good. May good fortune be theirs, and may they never desert the embrace of their beloved asses and the delights of their dialectics. I am forcing no one, and even if I wanted to, I could not. I merely warn and give exhortation, and, as befits a philosopher, say freely what I think. Perhaps at some time in the future they will be convinced, and they will realize that my admonitions were well-intended, but then it will do them no good, except that in their wisdom, so lately arrived at, they may advise those younger than themselves to become wise sooner.

Yet I testify by my own conscience and by the great and good God, who sees and hears all of this, that I am astounded to think that anyone could condemn what I say if he were to understand it properly. I do not think there is anyone in the whole world, learned or unlearned, genius or simpleton, who would not be convinced of my words if he could be made to understand them. But our generation does not like to hear such things. I wish them to know that I do not look to their opinion, which is of no importance, but to the attitude of learned men, who are not numerous, certainly, but whose prestige is much greater. It is they that I am eager to please, and I do not care to count opinions, but to weigh them. Young men do not like what I have to say, for they have neither wisdom, judgement, nor intelligence, but older men give me their approbation, since their years have given them a better sense of judgement. As for our Spanish countrymen, I do not merely warn and exhort them, but I implore and beseech them by all that is holy that they put an end to their delirious foolishness and that they dedicate their fine talents to the study of beautiful things, so that just as we are superior to all other nations in our resources of talent, so we may also be in learning, which certainly behooves our talents. This discussion is a very far-reaching one, and for that reason this letter has been more prolix than I thought. Indeed if I did not restrain myself, I should have gone on much further, swept along by my argument. But this letter must come to an end at some time, and I shall not exhaust all my thought, so that if in

plerosque ipsorum offensura. Ab unoquoque tamen eorum qui
offendentur, hoc me impetrare aequum est, ut credat me non esse
peculiariter de se locutum, neue ipsum uerba moueant, rem potius
perpendat, & animum meum. Quod si haec illi omnia parum
5 probantur, ego aequi bonique facio, & quod sit ei faustum &
felix, haereat in complexu suorum perquam suauium asinorum,
suaeque lepidae dialecticae. Ego neminem cogo, ac neque si uellem,
possem quidem. Moneo atque hortor, & ut philosophum decet,
libere quae sentio dico. Quae tamen ipsi aliquando probabunt, &
10 me bene monuisse tunc sentient, cum nihil eis ita sentire profuerit,
cumque ipsi sero sapuerint, iunioribus tamen consulent, ut maturius
sapiant.

Quanquam testor conscientiam meam, & Deum Optimum
Maximum, qui haec omnia uidet auditque, mirari me, quenquam
15 fore, qui haec modo intelligat, damnet. Neque enim arbitror
aliquem esse in toto orbe, siue doctum, siue inscium, siue ingenio-
sum, siue hebetem stupidumque, cui haec non probentur, si ita
dicantur, ut ipse intelligat. Verum nostris hominibus parum haec
modo placent; at ego non eorum iudicium, quod nullius momenti
20 est, sed doctorum illud, non numerosum quidem, ceterum amplis-
simum atque grauissimum specto, illique placere studeo. Neque
enim numerare sententias soleo, sed appendere. Non placeo iuueni-
bus, quibus nullum est consilium, nullum iudicium, nulla mens.
At senibus placebo, cum illis aetas melioris iudicii nonnihil attulerit.
25 Nostros tamen Hispanos non tam moneo & hortor, quam per
quicquid est sacrorum obtestor obsecroque, ut finem iam faciant
ineptiendi ac delirandi, pulcherrima ingenia studio dedant rerum
pulcherrimarum, ut quemadmodum multis dotibus sumus ceteris
gentibus superiores, ita & simus eruditione, quae si aliqua ingenia
30 decet, nostra profecto decet. Verum huiusce rei argumentum latis-
simum est. Idcirco prolixior opinione mea fuit epistola, & nisi
me retinuissem, labebar ducente oratione multo longius. Sed finem
aliquando tandem epistolae fieri necesse est. Nec omnia semel

---

7 lepidae] festivae S   9 sentio] sentiam S

the future there be further debate on this issue, I shall return to the fray with renewed vigor. There will be no lack of ammunition, thanks to the enormity of this madness, nourished and coddled as it has been for so many years.

Before I finish, I cannot help admonishing the reader again, if there will be any other reader beside yourself, not to read this letter already convinced and carried off in the opposite direction by some mental confusion, but to submit the whole matter to the examination of reason. If my argument seems convincing, let him follow my advice, but if not, I hope that he will praise my good intentions, and will interpret my words in a good sense. Just as I should wish my warnings to be accepted by others, so I should be willing to receive your advice or the advice of anyone else. If there is anyone who is not convinced by what I say, I should like very much to hear his opinion, and likewise, if there is some difficulty of interpretation, something that holds up his understanding, some scruple, my work is ready for him for the public good, provided that it is not simply for dispute, but for seeking out the truth. Otherwise there will never be an end to these disputes. But if they are so ardent for the fight, I am also prepared to engage their strongest gladiator in battle, and shall not shrink back from the arena or the playing field, that I may satisfy the wishes of my friends in every respect.

I had just finished this letter to you when Peter Gratian Laloo and my good friends (who I hope will soon also be yours) Toussaint Hosey and Nicolas Wotton came to see me.[90] They are much taken with you, even if they have not seen you, basing their judgement on what I have told them about your good qualities. They all asked me to send you their personal greetings, Laloo as our friend of long standing, and Hosey and Wotton, soon to be your friends. Greetings also from Nicolas Valdaura, a close relative of mine, whom I commend to you with the highest regard, as I have done on other occasions (as you know, he is as dear to me as a brother). Give my regards to Davalus also. Goodbye, my dearest friend, Fort.

Louvain
February 13, 1519

effundam, ut si saepius decertandum sit, quod futurum non dubito, nouus semper ueniam, quam facultatem magnitudo istius stultitiae tot iam annos molliter atque indulgenter enutritae & auctae mihi largitur.

5 Illud tamen antequam finiam non admonere rursus lectorem non possum, si modo quisquam erit huius rei, praeter te, lector, ut has ipse litteras, non a perturbatione aliqua sui animi in contrarium persuasus & raptus legat, sed rationis examine cuncta perpendat. Si ipsi bene suadere uidebor, consilium sequatur meum, sin uero 10 secus, animum prodesse cupientem laudet, uerba uero consulat boni. Atque ego quo animo ab aliis admonitionem hanc meam accipi uellem, eodem etiam aliorum, siue tuam, siue quis alius me admonere uoluerit, capiam. Ita, si quis est, cui haec quae dico minus probantur, eius ego perlibenter sententiam audiero. Sin uero 15 quidpiam ex iis, quae diximus, aliquis ambigit, si quo loco haeret, si quid eum remoratur, si aliquis etiam num urget scrupus, ei quoque publici commodi gratia, opera mea parata est, modo id non litigandi, sed inquirendae ueritatis causa fiat. Nam alioqui nunquam finis contentionum inueniretur. Quod si tantus illi fuerit pugnandi 20 ardor, ego etiam, ut per omnia meis istis amicis obsequar, uel cum fortissimo eorum Thrace comparatus, arenam & campum non refugiam. Haec tibi cum scripsissem, uenerunt ad me Petrus Gratianus Lalous noster, & Toussanus Hocedius, Nicolausque Votonius, nunc mei, breui quoque, ut spero, tui. Mire enim te etsi 25 nunquam a se uisum diligunt, ducti iis rebus, quas illis ego de uirtute retuli tua, omnes iusserunt salutem hic tibi nomine suo adscribi. Lalous quidem, ut iam pridem communis amicus, Hocedius uero, & Votonius, ut breui futuri. Nicolao Valdaurae, consanguineo meo, S. quem tibi, quod & saepe alias feci, quam possum maxime 30 commendo. Est enim mihi, ut scis, non minus carus, quam frater. Daualum quoque pro me saluta. Vale, mi suauissime Fortis. Louanii, Idibus Februariis, M.D. XIX.

---

30 frater] *add.* Poblationi nostro uiro summa & eruditione & integritate praedito, multam meis uerbis S

---

[90] Laloo was at Louvain together with Vives when he wrote the *In pseudodialecticos*. Toussaint Hosey of Valenciennes was a student at the *Trilingue* and became Bishop of Toul in 1543. Nicholas Wotton, the famous Tudor diplomat, secretary of state and Dean of Canterbury, was a friend of Vives in student days.

BIBLIOGRAPHY

Bataillon, Marcel. *Erasmo y España*, trans. Antonio Latorre. 2 vols. México: Fondo de Cultura Económica, 1966.
——. "Vives, réformateur de la bienfaisance" *Bibliothèque d'humanisme et Renaissance*, 14, (1952), 141-158.
Bochénski, Innocentius M. *A History of Formal Logic*, tr. I. Thomas. Notre Dame: University Press, 1961.
Boehner, Philotheus. *Medieval Logic: An Outline of Its Development from 1250-c. 1400*. Manchester: University Press, 1952.
Bonilla y San Martín, Adolfo. *Luis Vives y la filosofía del Renacimiento*. 2 vols., Madrid: Nueva Biblioteca Filosófica, 1929.
Burleigh, Walter. *De puritae artis logicae tractatus longior*, ed. P. Boehner. St. Bonaventure: Franciscan Institute, 1955.
Bussche, Emile van den. "Mémoire sur la vie et les écrits de Jean Louis Vives" *Mémoires couronnées de l'Académie Royale des Sciences et Belles-Lettres de Bruxelles*, 15. Brussels, 1841, 13-35.
Cassirer, Ernst, Oscar Kristeller, John Randall. *The Renaissance Philosophy of Man*. Chicago: University of Chicago Press, 1948.
Erasmus. *The Correspondence of Erasmus*, eds. W. K. Ferguson, R. A. B. Mynors, D. F. S. Thomson. Vol. I. Toronto: University of Toronto Press, 1974.
——. *Opus Epistolarum Des. Erasmi Roterodami*, eds. P. S., H. M. Allen and H. W. Garrod, 12 vols., Oxford: Clarendon, 1906-1958.
——. *Praise of Folly*, trans. Betty Radice. Harmondsworth: Penguin, 1971.
Esterlich, J. *Vives Exposition organisée à la Bibliothèque Nationale*. Paris, 1941.
Faludy, György. *Erasmus of Rotterdam*. London: Eyre and Spottiswoode, 1970.
Grabmann, Martin. "Die Sophismatenliteratur des 12. Jahrhunderts" *Beiträge zur Geschichte der Philosophie und Theologie des Mittelalters*, Bd. 38, H. I. Münster: Aschendorff, 1940
Guerlac, Rita. "Vives and the Education of Gargantua," *Etudes Rabelaisiennes* (Geneva, 1974), pp. 63-72.
Hutten, Ulrich von. *Epistolae Obscurorum Vivorum*, ed. Francis G. Stokes. London: Chatto and Windus, 1925.
Kneale, William and Martha. *The Development of Logic*. Oxford: Clarendon, 1906.
Kretzmann, Norman. *William of Sherwood's Introduction to Logic. Translated with an Introduction and Notes*. Minneapolis: University of Minnesota Press, 1966.
——. *William of Sherwood's Treatise on Syncategorematic Words*. Minneapolis: University of Minnesota Press, 1968.
McConica, James Kelsey. *English Humanists and Reformation Politics under Henry VIII and Edward VI*. Oxford: Clarendon, 1965.
Minio-Paluello, L. *Twelfth Century Logic: Texts and Studies*. 2 vols. Roma: Edizioni di storia e letteratura, 1956-1958.
Moody, Ernest Addison. *The Logic of William of Ockham*. London: Sheed and Ward, 1935.

——. *Truth and Consequence in Medieval Logic. Studies in Logic and the Foundations of Mathematics.* Amsterdam: North-Holland, 1953.
——. *Studies in Medieval Philosophy, Science and Logic* (Berkeley, 1975), pp. 371-392.
Monsegú, Bernardo. *Filosofía del humanismo de Juan Luis Vives.* Madrid: Consejo Superior de Investigaciones Científicas, 1961.
Noreña, Carlos. *Juan Luis Vives.* The Hague: Nijhoff, 1970.
Ong, Walter J. *Ramus, Method, and the Decay of Dialogue.* Cambridge: Harvard University Press, 1958.
Peter of Spain. *Summulae logicales,* ed. I. M. Bochénski. Turin: Marietti, 1947.
——. *The Summulae Logicales of Peter of Spain,* ed. J. P. Mullaly. Notre Dame: University Press, 1945.
——. *Tractatus,* ed. J. M. de Rijk. Assen: Van Gorcum, 1972.
——. *Tractatus syncategorematum,* tr. J. P. Mullaly. Milwaukee: Marquette University Press, 1964.
Pinta y Llorente, Miguel, and José M. de Palacio. *Procesos inquisitoriales contra la familia judía de Luis Vives.* Madrid: Consejo Superior de Investigaciones Científicas, 1964.
Poliziano, Angelo. *Le selve e la strega,* ed. Isidoro del Lungo. Firenze: Sansoni, 1925.
Prantl, Carl. *Geschichte der Logik im Abendlande.* 4 vols. in 2. Leipzig: Gustav Fock, 1927.
Puigdollers, Mariano. *La filosofía española de Juan Luis Vives.* Barcelona: Editorial Labor, 1940.
Rashdall, Hastings. *The Universities of Europe in the Middle Ages,* ed. F. M. Powicke and A. B. Emden. 3 vols. Oxford: Clarendon, 1936.
Renaudet, Augustin. *Préréforme et Humanisme à Paris pendant les premières guerres d'Italie.* 2nd. ed., Paris: Librairie d'Argences, 1951.
——. *Humanisme et Renaissance.* Genève: Librairie Droz, 1958.
Rogers, Elizabeth Frances. *Sir Thomas More, Selected Letters.* New Haven: Yale University Press, 1961.
de Rijk, Lambertus Maria. *Logica modernorum: A Contribution to the History of Early Terminist Logic,* Vol. I. *On the Twelfth Century Theories of Fallacy.* Assen: Van Gorcum, 1962.
——. *Logica modernorum: A Contribution to the History of Early Terminist Logic,* Vol. II. *The Origin and Early Development of the Theory of Supposition,* Parts One and Two. Assen: Van Gorcum, 1967.
Sancipriano, Mario. *Il pensiero psicologico e morale di G. L. Vives.* Firenze: Sansoni, 1957.
Spade, Paul Vincent. "Five Logical Tracts by Richard Lavenham" in *Essays in Honour of Charles Anton Pegis,* ed. J. Reginald O'Donnell. 70-124. Toronto: Pontifical Institute of Mediaeval Studies, 1974.
——. "The Origins of Medieval Insolubilia Literature," *Franciscan Studies.* 1973, 292-309.
Stenberghen, Fernand van. *Aristotle in the West: The Origins of Latin Aristotelianism,* tr. L. Johnston. Louvain: E. Nauwelaerts, 1955.
Vasoli, Cesare. "Giovanni Ludovico Vives e la polemica antiscolastica nello 'In pseudodialecticos,' " *Miscelánea de estudios a Joaquín Carvalho.* 7, (1961), 679-686.
——. *La dialettica e la retorica dell'umanesimo.* Milano: Feltrinelli, 1968.
Villoslada, R. G. *La Universidad de París durante los estudios de Francisco de Vitoria,* 1507-1522, Analecta gregoriana, 14, 159-177.

Vives, Juan Luis. *Joannis Ludovici Vivis Valentini Opera*. Basel, 1555.
——. *Joannis Ludovici Valentini Opera Omnia*, ed. Gregorio Mayáns y Síscar. 8 vols., Valencia, 1782. Reprint, London: Gregg Press Ltd., 1964.
——. *Obras completas*, ed. Lorenzo Riber, 2 vols. Madrid: Aguilar, 1947.
——. *Diversa opuscula*. Basel, 1538.
——. *Opuscula varia*. Louvain, 1519.
——. *De subventione pauperum*, ed. Armando Saitta. Firenze: La Nuova Italia, 1973.
——. *Adversus pseudo-dialecticos. Pompeius fugiens*. Sélestat, 1520.
——. *Vives' Introduction to Wisdom, A Renaissance Textbook*, ed. Marian Tobriner. New York: Teachers' College Press, 1968.
Vocht, Henry de. *Monumenta Historia Lovaniensia*. Louvain: Librairie universitaire, 1934.
——. *History of the Foundation and Rise of the Collegium Trilingue Lovaniense*. Louvain: Librairie universitaire, 1951-55.
——. *Literae virorum eruditorum ad Franciscum Craneveldium*. Louvain: Librairie universitaire, 1929.
Watson, Foster. *Vives and the Renascence Education of Women*. New York: Longmans, Green and Co., 1912.
——. "The Father of Modern Psychology" *Psychological Review* 22 (1915), 333-353.
——. *Luis Vives el Gran Valenciano*. Valencia, 1923.
Wilson, Curtis. *William Heytesbury: Medieval Logic and the Rise of Mathematical Physics*. Madison: University of Wisconsin Press, 1956.

INDEX OF NAMES AND SUBJECTS